MORE POWER TO YOU

By the same author:

More Power to You

MERLIN CAROTHERS

KINGSWAY PUBLICATIONS
EASTBOURNE

ISBN 0 85476 424 0

Distributed in India by OM Books, Secunderabad.

Produced by Bookprint Creative Services
P.O. Box 827, BN23 6NX, England for
KINGSWAY PUBLICATIONS LTD
Lottbridge Drove, Eastbourne, E Sussex BN23 6NT.
Printed in Great Britain

TABLE OF CONTENTS

Introduction

MORE POWER TO YOU

If my car won't start, I always get out and check under the hood. That's what you're supposed to do, isn't it? I check to see if the engine is still there. If it is, I'm lost.

I do know how to look around and see if a tow truck just happens to be passing by. But how to put the power back into the engine to get me where I want to go — that's a mystery!

However, I have discovered the source and learned how to put another kind of power into my life. Power to enjoy life whether the car engine is working or not. Power to be happy, even if I don't have a car. Power to be at peace if I have the best car made, and other cars get in my way, bump into me, or (Heaven forbid) scratch the finish!

But if you aren't having trouble with your car, how would you feel if suddenly confronted by a vicious-looking German Shepherd dog, charging at you with the obvious intention of sinking his teeth into you? Would you feel helpless . . . powerless? If so, in panic you might turn and run. But this would be exactly the wrong thing to do. Dogs love to chase people, especially anyone who shows fear. What should you do? You have power to control the dog. But you have to know how to use it.

Instead of following the instinct to run, (and who could outrun a big dog?) we should move toward it. That's right. *Toward* it. And in a loud, commanding voice shout, "Down!" or "You bad dog!"

In every problem God has provided us a solution, but even His solution is useless unless we know what it is and how to use it. God has been teaching me many new things and I want to share them with you so that when problems and calamities attack, you will be ready. This power is available to every one of us.

1

GOD CHANGES PEOPLE

I needed to change. But that understanding was far from me that black night I now relive in memory . . .

Drawing a bandanna across my face, over nose and mouth, tying a knot behind my head, I didn't really care who saw my face. But a warning light flashed somewhere in the back of my mind. So without knowing why, I decided to keep my face covered.

I gripped my M-l army rifle, smashing the butt against the window. Moving swiftly now, I unlocked, then raised the window and dove through. I knew I had to be swift before the occupants of the house had time to get a weapon to defend themselves or run for help. With a few quick strides, I raced through the unoccupied room and crashed through the doorway, into the family living room.

Only seconds had passed since the smashing of the window. The entire family sat stock-still in their chairs as the violent American GI suddenly exploded into the quiet of their family gathering. He was masked, clutching an ominous-looking rifle. They were too frightened to even scream.

World War II had ended only months earlier. We who had been bombed, starved, frozen, living to kill or be killed, were now the designated servants of peace. Germany was crushed and helpless. But I was still an angry young man.

I had seen members of my own 82nd Airborne Division hanging by their feet, bodies riddled with machine bullets. These were the sad victims of the infamous SS troops. A violent hatred existed between the Nazi SS and U.S. paratroopers.

But for me, anger had not started on the battlefields of Belgium and Germany. It was merely an opportunity to express an already deep-seated anger. It festered within me like an ugly boil trying to break through the skin.

I was angry with God, myself and others. I had no more reason to be angry than millions of other men on both sides of the war. But another man's anger was his. Mine was mine. My motto was, "Take care of number one."

Taking care of number one at the moment meant getting a radio. We who had won the war had no radios. But the local German families did. They occasionally played them loud enough for us to hear! The solution seemed simple enough to me. They had what I wanted, so I would go out and get it.

The fact that the U.S. Government did not allow us to take anything from the German people didn't phase me. As far as I was concerned, the "Government" hadn't supplied me with a radio, so I would take one.

And take one I did. Waving my rifle, I directed everyone in the room to stand against the wall. The cold, violent anger in my eyes spoke volumes. One wrong move and I could easily add a few more casualties to an already finished war.

2

Without a word I backed toward the door, radio in one arm, and quickly exited out the window. In a few seconds, I was swallowed up in the blackness of the night and on my way back to the army camp. The entire episode had lasted barely more than sixty seconds ...

This incident represented more than one man's anger and hostility at the futility of war and hatred for the injustices of it all. Most of all, it represented an attitude of mind and heart.

I was running from God, and the harder I ran the greater the anger that grew within. People were my enemies and I was prepared to challenge anyone who crossed me.

Anger, remorse, anxiety and frustration are almost always the result of believing we should have more than we do. More money, more health, more pleasure, more recognition, more comfort from others . And that is basically the problem with human nature. We want what we want, when we want it and how we want it!

God says, "I promised to supply all your needs."

But God's promises seem too distant and vague to satisfy us.

At one time I found myself arguing with God, "But God, I asked you for help yesterday, and the day before that, and ... how can I trust You if I'm still in this mess?"

"What mess?"

"All this trouble and these problems and these needs."

"You have what you need. I have personally made sure of it."

"Well then, God, I don't understand You. If I were You and You were me, I would have made life a whole lot easier for You than You have made it for me."

"I wanted life to be so much easier for you that I gave My only Son for you. He came to change you into the kind of person I first created you to be. But you don't want to change. You only want your way."

"But God, I do want to change. If You would help me, I would get better."

3

"I am helping you. Every experience you are going through has been carefully designed to help you. I promise to supply what you need and will never fail to keep My Word to you. But your ears are dull of hearing. I have told you to be anxious for nothing. But you must not be hearing Me, for you are anxious about many things."

"But God, I am anxious only because my prayers never seem to be answered."

"You are not praying right."

"But I am praying the best I know how."

"Stop your much praying and learn to pray as My Son did. His prayer was, 'Not my will but Thine be done.' Pray like this and you will never be disappointed again."

***

How patiently and kindly God strives to change us. Along with feelings, desires, ambitions, responses and attitudes, the entire personality needs to be changed. And God is in the changing business. He is looking for people who want to be changed. He was once sorry He ever created man, but He decided to invest everything He was and everything He had in re-creating us into something He would be pleased with. It might take Him all eternity to make something good out of us but He will never give up.

I came to Him. And I keep coming back to Him and seeking to be changed ... continually. The more He changes me the more I can see how wrong I was the day before. The wonder of it all is that I *can* be changed. All of us can be changed. It doesn't even matter how far away from God we are right now.

The Prodigal Son was very far away from his father. He had completely disregarded all of his father's desires and good plans for his life. He had foolishly wasted everything his father had given him. His father stood aside and let him do as he would and the son worked his way clear to the bottom. As our young people say today, "It was the pits."

Well, when we are at the bottom of the heap, the only

way we can go is up. So the son made a decision to *change his direction* in life. Climbing out of the pigpen, he started home to his father.

Remember, his father saw him from a long way off ... and he ran to meet him. The father had not yet heard the son asking for forgiveness or making any promises to be a better man. For all he knew, he might just be coming back to ask for more money! But he rejoiced that the son was headed in the right direction ... home.

Jesus told this story to illustrate God's attitude toward you and me. He is not concerned about *where we are* when we realize our need — the lack in our spiritual lives — as long as we start moving in the right direction, *toward Him*.

"Well, God isn't going to get much when He gets me," you may be thinking. If you think you're a hard nut to crack, rejoice. St. Paul was too. And look what God was able to do with his life.

Just as a sculptor takes an ugly stone and carves out a thing of beauty, God carved a monument of strength and faith out of Paul of Tarsus, a man who was seeking to destroy faith in Jesus. Paul became a great man. So you see, God can take the roughest material and create something which will be the most enduring. The more He changes us, the more glory He receives. For the work of art, that the sculptor carves from rough stone, is to his glory.

You may think that you are one of God's harder rocks! But forget about what you are and start concentrating on what He is doing with you. It may be painful, but that's because of what you are. It may take longer for God to change you than it does to change anyone else. But remember, hard rocks make the most beautiful statues.

If you feel He is spending a lot of time chipping away at your rough edges, remember that He is putting you through a necessary refining process, and you will be feeling the pressure and stress that are a part of the process.

It's a little like the blacksmith who examines a piece of iron and decides what has to be done to make it useful. He heats it white hot, and when he places it on the anvil he knows just the amount of pressure, pounding and flattening it can withstand, as he carefully prepares it for its intended use.

I think of God as the blacksmith and myself as the piece of iron. God knows the changes that need to be made in me for my good and He uses many events to shape me. But since I know God is in charge of the entire process, I can rejoice over what He wants to create in me. He knows what He is doing!

II

CHANGE ME! CHANGE ME!

Change me, change me, change me!

Nearly everyone wants to be different. Tall people want to be shorter. Short people want to be taller. Fat people want to be thinner. Thin people think they are too skinny. Rich people wish they had more freedom from the responsibilities of wealth. People struggling to make ends meet would change places in a minute! Students want to get out of school. Many non-students say those were the best days of their lives, and wish they could get back in.

Is there any one satisfied with who he is and where he's at in life? It doesn't seem so, does it?

In more than one society from the past, white was beautiful. It signified being part of the culturally elite. In our day people bake in the sun for hours, just to keep from having that pasty, white look!

Times change. But dissatisfaction with self doesn't. It robs us of the real *joy* of living.

***

In 1943, I was lying on the wet, cold ground, clutching a rebellious rifle that just wouldn't shoot exactly where I wanted it to! I wasn't very pleased with myself.

Other soldiers lay beside me on the same firing range but I felt very much alone. So far as I could tell, I was doing my very best, but it didn't seem to be good enough.

And besides, what difference did it make? I was too cold, too disgusted to care. One part of me wanted to become the best marksman in the regiment. The other part? Well ... no prior experience at firing a rifle, no one cared whether I did or not ... I had never come out first place in anything before. Who would care if I did?

I felt a tap on my shoulder. When I looked up, to my surprise, I saw the gold bars of our second lieutenant platoon leader.

"Carothers, I've been watching you."

"Oh, no," I thought. "Now I'm going to get it. He's seen how badly I'm doing."

"You could become the best marksman in the company, maybe the regiment."

With that he was gone.

I turned on my side and watched him walk back to the company commander's tent.

"He was serious," I thought. But how could he be serious? I didn't have it in me to be the best marksman ... or did I?

Then I began to try in earnest. The lieutenant had said I could, so maybe I could. I gave it my best, and I did! He had changed my image of myself.

Years later, I felt another tap on my shoulder. This time it was Jesus. He saw a potential for my life. He said I could become a new man, if I wanted, because He could change me. I wanted and He did.

But the effects of the change Jesus made in me proved to be much more far-reaching and satisfying than the effects of winning a rifle match. I didn't realize all that happened when He came into my life. It wasn't clear to me that I would never again be all alone. I didn't understand what power He wanted to give me. Nor was it clear that through Him I could do all things. "All things?" Step by step I'm realizing what "all things" are and the unlimited power available to change me — mold me — make me what I should be. Power to make me more of what He would like me to be. Power to help others.

In a recent survey, a group of wives whose average age was thirty years, were asked to rate in order of severity the problems a wife and mother commonly faces: finances, sex, in-laws, fatigue, aging, loneliness and low opinion of self. They ranked one item far above all the rest as the greatest source of suffering in their lives. It was not surprising to find that it was "low opinion of self".

The records of men given dishonorable discharges from the American Armed Forces reveals an amazing common denominator. They had a very poor regard for themselves. Usually they tried to conceal their sense of inferiority by bragging and acting tough. An examination of their records, however, revealed they seldom listed themselves as outstanding in either sports, academics, hobbies, skills or personal achievement. They were people who needed help, but who refused to face their need honestly.

We can endure great stress and pain as long as we have a healthy estimate of our own worth. But stripped of this, we become prime prospects for perpetual misery. We become people in need of help.

Behavioral scientists believe the stage can be set for success or failure from the first years of life by those who are instrumental in reinforcing a negative or positive self-image — our parents.

One individual who made recent history bears out the truth of this. His actions culminated in tragedy that touched the lives of all of us and ended in his own destruction. A look into his background is revealing.

His mother was so masculine that she regularly beat up her first husband. He divorced her. She married again, but her second husband divorced her also. He, too, grew tired of his wife's assault and battery. It was by her third husband that she conceived and bore the child whose life illustrates the truth about our feelings of self-worth and how our parents can affect those feelings. When the third husband died of a heart attack, the mother was forced to support her son alone. She apparently had little love for him, and even when he was still quite young, did her best to avoid his company. She stayed at home while he was in school and worked when he was at home. Her son grew up believing he was unlovable, unwanted and useless. This young man eventually became well-known all over the world. His name was Lee Harvey Oswald.

Millions of hours of lost sleep and of lives drained of energy result directly from the way people feel sorry for themselves. I once felt so sorry for myself that I wished I would die. Later I learned that the very experience which had made me want to die had actually worked out *for my good*. All my self-pity had done nothing but make me miserable.

Training to be happy with one's self begins very early. I recall looking into the mirror every morning and wishing my appearance were different. My hair was much too nondescript — no class. My face wasn't masculine. In fact nothing about me was worthy of special mention. But I was stuck with "me". So there seemed little I could do but feel sorry for myself.

In the midst of such dark thoughts, a little light broke through as I began to think, "I didn't create myself. So I can't take the blame. God made me. But if I blame Him I might be in trouble. Surely He must have known what He was doing when He designed my features. The way I look is part of His plan."

So I began to re-evaluate "me". My hair started looking better — well, at least less "icky". My ears weren't the glaring defect I had thought. My chin might even be a subtle sign of intelligence rather than a lack of masculinity. As I began to see myself as God's creation, I could even smile at myself. I didn't have to blame myself or God for what I was. Maybe, if I stopped feeling sorry for myself, He could do something with what He had created. To trust Him was a necessary ingredient in His recipe for success.

All of us are equipped to do something. God gave us more abilities than any of us will completely use in our lifetime! A man who has never attended college may be able to sway a huge crowd while he holds their rapt attention for an hour. Another speaker may be rich in education and experience, but his audience may be full of people suppressing yawns . . . soon, there will be no one left to bore.

The first man refused to be handicapped by his lack. He took the little that he had and moved forward with it.

We shouldn't complain because people respond to us negatively. Instead we should find out *why* they do. And we need to find out what will cause them to respond more positively. God has equipped us with all we need to move people or mountains.

Whenever we fail to hold the attention of other people, or to convince them to believe as we do, we might be tempted to think, "Such dense people don't have enough sense to appreciate the important things I'm trying to share with them. So I will leave them alone." Or perhaps we become so discouraged that we give up. But that isn't the answer. Blaming others or giving up doesn't accomplish anything.

Jesus told the disciples to follow Him and He would make them fishers of men. He didn't say He would make people follow them. They were to learn how to draw others *to* them. A wise fisherman never blames the fish for not taking his bait nor swimming into his net. He learns what bait will attract the most fish or where to place his net. A wise man doesn't waste his time worrying why success isn't knocking at his door demanding to be let in. Instead he faces his failure squarely and finds out what he can do, then learns to do it well.

An individual is fired for not pleasing the boss. An angry, frustrated, jobless person might react, "Stupid man! Can't he see I know how to do the job better than he does?"

Or, "Why don't I ever get the breaks?"

A man complains year after year because he's given neither a raise nor a promotion. Others pass him by. He is convinced they know far less about the business than he does. He may even work harder than they do. Still, he gets passed by.

It has been said, "If you work hard, you will always get ahead." But that is not the whole truth. Some people drive themselves frantically and never get ahead. Why? They fail to properly use the resources God has given them. They may even have failed to recognize the resources themselves.

Jesus said, "Come follow Me, and I will teach you." His invitation is to everyone. Everyone can learn! Power to be a people-mover is available. But it is from Him.

The handful of men who learned under the Master went out and turned the then-known world upside down. They learned to be "fishers of men." We have the same good news to share with a world that needs help.

It's imperative that we learn how to influence others for His sake. A good place to begin could well be in our own back yard. A wife complains because her husband forgets her birthday or their anniversary. After many forgotten birthdays, she feels rejected, neglected, unloved. He grows to hate himself or may feel, "If she were a better wife, I wouldn't be so forgetful." What should a wife do?

She should do as my wife, Mary, does. She gets out my calendar notebook and writes in her birthday and our anniversary. A month ahead of time she reminds me of the coming special date and what she would enjoy receiving. Then a week ahead she reminds me and maybe even the day before. She always does this in a loving, thoughtful way. She makes it easy for me to remember. Birthdays and anniversaries end up happy because Mary is finding solutions rather than problems. She makes me feel good by her faithfulness in reminding me and I make her feel good by doing what I can to make the occasion enjoyable.

But the man who prays, "Lord, change my wife so she will love me," may be wasting his time. God is not going to answer a prayer like that if the man is not responding to his wife's needs. If the husband has failed to learn what his wife needs, that is the *real problem*.

This man can moan and groan all he wants because God doesn't seem to be helping him.

Rather, let him pray in this manner:

"Thank you, Lord, that I am in this situation. I know there is something I am supposed to learn. Now teach me, Lord, what it is that I need to do that will please my wife. And thank you, Lord, for providing me with an opportunity to grow in the way You know is best."

This kind of praying works. It produces power in us. And we become "people influencers" — leaders, teachers, writers, developers of happy people, sharers of life! — "fishers of men."

Many marriages are destroyed by husbands or wives who persistently point out what is wrong with their spouses. Every person wants to feel that he is his own person, a unique individual. But constant fault-finding tends to undermine this feeling of individuality. How can anyone retain it if he or she keeps hearing, "If I've told you once, I've told you a million times."?

Telling others "one more time" becomes a compulsion. Why tell anyone anything if it does no good? Why drive children out of the home by repeating the same things to them in the same way, over and over?

Jesus told Peter, "Let your net down on the other side." Peter could have argued. Instead he listened. He learned. He also caught fish.

We all need to be willing to change in order to fit into *His plan*. We all need more power to be successful at whatever it is we are trying to do. And it is available.

Do you want a change in your life? God wants a change, too. He wants to see us changed into the image and likeness of His Son. That takes a power that goes beyond our own resources. The beautiful part of it is, that power *is available* and God desires to fill our lives with it.

III

GOD LOVES ME

Pastor Blake found it hard to rejoice. Forces beyond his control seemed to be pounding against him from every direction and he finally cried out to the Lord, "I need help!"

"Lord, my body is sick and tired."

"My bills are so late being paid, I'm ashamed to go out of the house."

"My family is falling apart."

"My life is a complete and total failure."

Breaking through his agony, he heard God speak to him for the first time in a long time. The voice within was so weak that he could barely hear what was being said.

"Do you know that I love you?"

When he recovered from the surprise of knowing God

was communicating with him, he said, "Yes, I know you do, Lord, but I need help."

If you knew I loved you, you would know that I am taking care of all your needs."

Instead of arguing about the message he was receiving, the pastor accepted it. To God and himself, he reaffirmed, "God loves me. He has to be taking care of me."

He told me that as he made this decision and declaration, the room seemed suddenly diffused with a warm glow. As he struggled with words to explain, he said,"Merlin, it was as if I had put my finger into an electric socket and current was flowing through me. I've never experienced anything like it. It was as if an electric current flowing through me were warming every part of my body and radiating out to warm the whole room."

This pastor had never been an overly emotional person. I could tell he chose his words carefully, for fear I would think he was exaggerating his experience. But I knew what had happened. He had reached a point in his life where he was about to blow a fuse. God knew he couldn't take any more and that his usefulness demanded a clear manifestation of His Presence.

The pastor went on to say that the more he believed God loved him, the warmer his body became. An ecstacy he had never known was suffusing his body because the simple truth of God's love — about which every Sunday School student sings — was becoming real to him by faith. As he increasingly affirmed that he knew God loved him, the power increased.

Then he said, "I reached a point where I believed I must surely be passing into the next world. I thought, 'If heaven is like this, it has to be glorious!' But I could see everything around me and couldn't understand how I could be dying and still be so very much alive. When it seemed as if my body couldn't withstand the force of energy flowing through me a second longer, it suddenly ceased. Everything was back to normal, except for a warm inner glow that stayed with me for hours."

This pastor's ministry was never the same after that. The

theme of his life and sermons became, "God loves you." His congregation, in fact everyone who met him, sensed that he knew something very special about God. Anxiety about problems he had labored under melted away.

Probably every one of us would like to stick our finger into God's "electric socket" and be instantly rejuvenated too. Rest assured, if He has an unusual experience planned for any of us, it will come. If not, the principle is still the same.

I've tried it over and over and it always works for me. When a problem bothers me, I concentrate on what I know is true. "God loves me." I feel no electric current, but the more I concentrate on His love for me, the more I know He is taking care of my "problems." And if He is taking care of them, why should I be troubled?

"Keep yourselves in the love of God." (Jude 21) This verse doesn't mean keep working at it so that you'll be worthy of God's love ... but always keep reminding yourself that *God loves you*. He is *always* for you. Keep yourself in His love by refusing to wander away into self-pity and despair.

A former pastor found himself writing to me from a prison cell. He had tried to cope with his "problems" in a way that produced harsh consequences. This former pastor, like Pastor Blake, had more burdens and problems than he could bear. His utter discouragement led him to commit crimes which he repeatedly justified to himself because he had so "many problems." He had wandered away from the love of God, having failed to learn the meaning of Jude 21.

I heard from him after he had ended up in prison with a ten-year sentence. He wrote, "When I came to myself here in prison, I cried,'God, what has happened to my life?' Instead of speaking to me directly, He let me receive a copy of your book, PRISON TO PRAISE. He taught me through your books that the key to a victorious Christian life is giving praise and thanks to God for everything."

The pastor is free now, living in Denver, and he wrote to me, "Now, when I invite someone to accept Christ, I merely tell them about the love and joy of Christ in me. His Spirit does the convicting, convincing and converting."

He knows God loves him, and that sort of underlying assurance affects his listeners more than the most eloquent and carefully thought-out arguments.

This man's story, like my own, illustrates again how God takes all that I do and uses it for some good(Romans 8:28), even if my own efforts are pitifully weak. Anyone who accepts the reality of God's love is changed — is continually *being changed and receives more power.*

Every problem that discourages us is, in some way, a consequence of not believing God really loves us. We can blame our problems on people, our situation or bad luck. But the truth is still the same. God loves us too much to take away any problem that has the potential of helping us.

Consider Helen Keller — blind, deaf and dumb. What good could possibly come from such difficult problems? Helen wrote,"I thank God for my handicaps, for through them I have found myself, my work, and my God." To find myself, my work and my God! What greater results can we hope to obtain?

It is when our burden seems heaviest that we feel the weakest. But this is just the time when we can receive His strength. This is what He meant when He told Paul, "In your weakness is My strength made perfect."

Perhaps the idea that God could be so personally involved in your life is completely new to you. But a God who knows the exact number of hairs on our heads is concerned with the small things that trouble us, as well as the big, overwhelming things that seek to crush us.

As we keep our focus on His love for us, we will find ourselves doing what God tells us in Jude 20: "Building up yourselves on your most holy faith."

Because God does love us in such a personal way, it should come as no surprise that He is also vitally interested in helping us to realize our need for a change. He will use our frustrations and dissatisfactions to help us see that need, too.

Who could dream that God would draw forth a revelation from the murky depths of the waters of Loch Ness in

Scotland to highlight the need for an in-depth change in me?

But that is just what He did ...

IV

ARE YOU LIKE LOCH NESS?

I held my breath. Any moment we might see it. The narrow road twisted and turned as it wound through the Scottish Highlands. Of course, I doubted the monster would appear today. That would be too much to expect. But then ... why not? Today was as good as any other day.

Maybe this was the day ...

Breathing in the bracing, chill air, I gazed out over the world famous Loch Ness. Enchanted with its smooth-as-glass surface reflecting a golden shimmer of sunlight, a question nudged my mind:

"How could a giant, prehistoric creature, the Loch Ness monster, live within the incredibly peaceful lake?"

But then, I was only scanning the surface. The lake is twenty-four miles long, varies in width from one to three miles, and is almost 1000 feet deep — more than twice the depth of the North Sea!

What lies beneath the surface?

A deep, dark mystery!

Only in recent years have scientists discovered that the 1000-foot-bottom of Loch Ness is not really the bottom. Scientists suspect that the lake goes even deeper, with subterranean channels connecting it to the Irish Sea. One of the discoveries they made was that it grew murkier as they penetrated more deeply. It became so murky that even the most powerful underwater lights devised by man could not penetrate it.

Somewhere within these incredibly deep regions are believed to live prehistoric creatures — behemoths that once roamed the earth by the thousands. For the past 1,500 years, individuals have reported sightings of the legendary Loch Ness monster, grey-black in color with a small dragon-like head, a long neck and usually trailing a series of undulating lumps behind it, breaking the stillness of the silent waters. The mysteries of Loch Ness, locked away in the depths, continue to elude man.

Many of us are similar to Loch Ness. The depths of our being remain hidden from sight, sometimes even from ourselves. We want to show our best face to the world, like the celebrity who wants to be photographed only from the "good side." But deep down inside, black layers of accumulated, repeated, unconfessed and unrenounced sources of guilt lurk, hidden in darkness too murky for the light of human understanding to penetrate. I saw how true this is during the course of a long-awaited trip abroad.

***

Mary and I had long wanted to visit England. But the opportunity had kept eluding us until May of 1978 when my schedule coincided marvelously with a charter flight. This trip would be unusual for us in another way. We were to have a vacation!

We boarded a Worldwide Tours charter plane in Los Angeles for a non-stop flight to England. Right over the top of the world! A heavy cloud covering kept us from getting a good look at the "top of the world," but we hoped for a clear view on the way back.

Arriving in Galwick Airport, south of London, at about 8:00 A.M. London time, we were a little groggy from traveling all night. Mary leaned against me for support and I leaned against her. Somehow we managed to get through customs and immigration. I had not been able to reserve a rental car ahead of time, so first off, we located a rental company and made arrangements for a medium sized four-door Ford. I was later thankful for its compact size. I could never have gotten a larger car through some of those narrow English lanes!

After loading up our luggage, I pulled the car out on the road.

"Let's see, now. Is this a one-way road or two-way?"

Everything looked peculiar sitting on the right side of the car with the gear shift on the left.

"Keep on the right side, Merlin." Mary cautioned me.

"No, here they drive on the left side."

"That's what I mean," Mary said. "Keep on the right side whichever side that is!"

"Let's not spend a lot of time in London," Mary suggested. "Let's get out of the city and into the English countryside. That's what I want to see!"

So we spent little time in London, just long enough to see some sights we agreed were essential. Our first stop was Big Ben. Mary had longed to see Big Ben ever since she was a little girl. Fortunately, we arrived only minutes before five o'clock in the evening. Standing beneath its tower, we breathlessly waited for the enormous clock to chime. At exactly five o'clock we were royally welcomed to London.

Bongg ... Bongg ...

It seemed as if the earth beneath our feet vibrated! Mary's face was transfixed with a rapt expression, her eyes shining as brightly as the diamonds in the Tower of London.

Bongg ... Bongg ... Bongg ... Big Ben's welcome seemed to rock us in the arms of time ...

Early next morning we set out to find Buckingham Palace, so we could watch the famous "Changing of the Guard." We made it on time. But so had several thousand others! The square was carpeted with wall-to-wall people. The press of the crowd was intense.

Finally the guards, resplendent in their historical and colorful uniforms, marched down the street and into the castle. But the mounted guards were more magnificent, with their shields and swords glistening in the early morning sun.

Within minutes, it was all over. Somehow we were able to get disentangled from the crowd and find our way back to our car.

Proceeding through a maze of narrow, twisted streets to the infamous Tower of London, our goal was to see the fabulous crown jewels which have been kept under guard at this site for the kings and queens of England for hundreds of years. Moving forward after a thirty-minute wait for admittance, we saw a sign just ahead, "CROWN JEWELS OF GREAT BRITAIN."

Would we really get near enough to touch them?

As the line approached this magnificent display, we were greeted by, "Keep moving, please!" No, we would not be allowed to touch them. For they were displayed behind heavy glass. But, even so, they were a sight not to be forgotten. I never realized how diamonds could shine. Many were as large as English walnuts.

We stood transfixed, not wanting to move. But soon came this inevitable, "Keep moving, please!"

I thought of heaven. It was a strange thought, as guards implored us to "move on." In heaven we will be able to spend as long as we want and see more beautiful scenes than we could ever imagine.

"Eye hath not seen, nor ear heard, the things God has prepared for those that love Him." (I Cor. 2:9)

As we made our way back to the car, I was thankful to realize there would be no hinderances to the fullness of joy we would experience in the Lord's presence. The brilliance of the crown jewels will pale next to the beauty He is preparing for us.

"What else would you like to see in London, Mary?"

"I know there is so much to see, but what I really want is to see the countryside!"

It wasn't an easy job getting out of London, but we persevered! In spite of bumper-to bumper traffic, a million honking horns and not a few angry taxicab drivers, we got out of London and headed for the open countryside.

And what countryside! Green grass. Really green grass. Rich. Deep. Lush. Green grass you have never seen the like of! And knee deep in the grass, sheep — hundreds of sheep — thousands of sheep! Their constant melody broke upon the quiet country air — "Ba-baa." "Ba-baa." They covered the side of the brilliantly green hills. We parked by the roadside and let our senses drink in the peace which surrounded us . . .

This was a real holiday! No schedules to keep. No place to get to. No one expecting us anywhere for two weeks. What luxury! As we cruised along each day without a care in the world, each new village was a fresh experience. And of course, each small village had its own pastry shop, beckoning us to visit awhile and sample the abundance of cakes, pastries, pies and candies.

Even though we didn't have to be in a hurry in our travels, we had a growing sense of urgency to reach one goal. Near Amesbury, England, on Salisbury Plain, lies an impressive prehistoric wonder known as Stonehenge.

Four thousand years ago, gigantic stones weighing twenty-five tons each, were moved by stalwart men of old and arranged in a horseshoe-shaped pattern, surrounded by a circle of smaller stones. Nineteen stones, twenty-two feet high weighing an estimated twenty-five tons each, had to be transported over one hundred miles. Engineers estimate that it would have taken one thousand men seven years to move just one of those mammoth stones that far.

Even more amazing than the transporting and placement of these stones is the astrological significance of

Stonehenge. All the stones were arranged so that the major axis points towards the rising sun at exactly mid-summer. Other astrological potentials built into the arrangements still puzzle scientists today.

Throughout forty centuries, untold thousands of persons have stopped to admire this monument, free to walk up and touch its ancient stones and marvel at its wonder, achieved totally without today's mechanical knowledge and technology.

Unfortunately, there have been those filled with hostility who senselessly destroy or desecrate things around them — public buildings, schools, churches, banks, art treasures, historic relics — even God's glorious and irreplaceable creations, those giant redwood trees that took a thousand or more years to grow.

This darkness in human hearts is making it necessary to remove priceless exhibits and certain national and inter-national monuments from close and direct view by the public. And thus we found it no different at Stonehenge.
. . .

As we drove the remaining two miles, the sky was filling with threatening black clouds. I breathed a silent prayer that God would hold them back just a little bit longer.

In only minutes we would be able to actually touch those ancient landmarks! As we approached, I thought, "Thank you, Lord. There is hardly anyone here. We will have it all to ourselves."

How disappointed we were to learn that due to malicious damage done to the stones, even to the painting of graffiti on them, officials were forced to stop everyone from getting close to them. All we could do was walk around the perimeter of Stonehenge and ponder from afar the mystery the stones held as they stood mute in their silent vigil. A barbed-wire fence now separates all visitors from direct access to this ancient wonder.

When I got over my initial disappointment, God showed me an important lesson. While the gigantic stones serve as a reminder of mysteries and marvels from the distant past, the barbed-wire fence is a reminder of unpleasant things to come. As the end-time approaches, mankind has become exactly as the Bible predicted: disrespectful, proud, haughty and irreverent.

Darkness and ugliness inside people wages war against the natural beauty created by God for all to see and enjoy. Therefore they cannot enjoy works of art by men and women who, created in His image, are moved to express this attribute of creativity.

God's divine light and beauty serve to remind us that darkness is a separation from Him. This darkness is driven to try to quench the light. Since it cannot do this, it destroys or reduces God-given or God-inspired beauty to the level of common ugliness.

At this point, my thoughts were drawn back to another mystery — the darkness in the depths of Loch Ness. I saw that at one time or another we are all somewhat like Loch Ness. Common to the condition of man is the dark side of human nature.

The age old question loomed before me, immovable as the silent giants of Stonehenge. What can we do to drain off the stagnant blackness of sin that lurks there and replace it with something fresh and vibrant? Something good.

Three simple effective things:

First — Recognize that hidden forces work within us. We may wish to see only the sparkling surface, but when we begin to plumb the depths, darkness begins to close in around us. At this point, we need to take a second step.

Second — Ask Christ to begin shedding light in the dark places. And even though the revelation of what is hiding in that darkness often makes us feel downright rotten, we are not to be sidetracked nor to stop.

We don't have to be afraid of what dark places are within us or what "Loch Ness monster" lurks beneath the surface of our lives if we know the power that is available to us. Some of my ancestors came from Scotland, so in a way, part of me was once in Scotland. Whatever my ancestors did is part of me. In some unfathomable way, I'm part of whatever they were. Sort of scary, isn't it? But

I'm also a part of what Jesus did! He released all the power of Heaven to change me. I'm still learning how glorious all that power is!

Once a transaction involving a considerable sum of God's money was troubling me. I questioned others' motives in how they were handling it. It seemed to me that they were not being completely honest with the people who gave the money. All the funds were being used for good, worthwhile purposes, but I kept feeling more money should be spent on the project I was most interested in. I worried about it. I lost sleep over it. There was darkness in me. Without doubt, I was questioning other people's motives. The harder I tried to let peace come into my heart, the more troubled I became. "Maybe I'm failing God. Maybe I should let them know what I think. Maybe I should take forceful steps to compel them to do what I believe is right. Maybe . . . "

Then it dawned on me. What would Jesus do? What would He want to do about it in me? Would He, who could create money in the mouth of a fish, be concerned over how money was spent so long as it was being used to help others? He would laugh at my anxiety. I could hear His clear, ringing voice, "What is it to you, Merlin? Follow Me!"

The power came on. The light banished the darkness! The problem was gone. The "monster" fled. I was at peace. The words He spoke two thousand years ago had changed me almost instantly. Instead of feeling anxious, I relaxed in the security of trusting Him to be in control.

Third — Let us believe God is doing a new thing in our lives. In His miraculous way, by revealing what has made life seem so cloudy and dark, the light is continually replacing the darkness — for darkness is the absence of light.

As we take these three simple steps, the light that has been touching only the surface of our lives begins to penetrate into the darkness at the lower levels of our being. The attitudes, habits and feelings that have made us so miserable are revealed for what they are . . . sin hidden by darkness.

And with the light comes new hope. Now I realize that the heaviness I have often felt inside and didn't understand, can be penetrated and dispelled by the perfect joy of Christ!

Again look at Jude 20 and 21 — "building up yourselves in your most holy faith, praying in the Holy Spirit. Keep yourselves in the love of God." (For He is able to keep you from falling and promises to present you blameless before the Father — Jude 24.)

Over and over I have seen in myself, and observed in many others, that bad habits — the tendencies to commit certain sins, the dark feelings that lurk beneath the surface — cannot resist constant praise and thanksgiving which will also keep us "in the love of God." Keep us daily in touch with and touched by His love. And I mean *constant* praise and thanksgiving. It is not enough to say:

"Well, God, I praised you for several days and nothing much happened, so let's call the whole thing off!"

No, we must praise the Lord daily, hourly...even continuously." (Ps.34:1) Then, even the most stubborn, bad habits or the darkest, hidden feelings will lose their grip on us.

Each word of praise we breathe gives God the opportunity to breathe new life into us — the opportunity to mold us a little more into the shape He desires our lives to take — a little more into the likeness of His Son.

With each offering of praise and thanksgiving...even though it be the "sacrifice of praise" (Heb.13:15) if need be, we will become less and less like the paradox of Loch Ness (sunlight on the surface and darkness in the depths) and more and more the way God intends us to be: *Sonlight all the way through!*

If we cling to some enjoyable sin or persist in our "right to feel miserable" even when we have invited the "light" into ourselves and are learning to praise the Lord continually — there is yet another thing we must consider.

We bring darkness into our own lives by our feelings towards others! When we harbor ill-feelings toward others, we effectively cut ourselves off from the source of power for the abundant and overcoming life. Mark 11:24-26 clearly says that those things which we desire, if we believe we receive them, we shall have them. But if we have unforgiveness in our heart, this is a negative attitude that remains hidden in darkness. As such, it disconnects us from our power source! Our negative feelings, attitudes and responses to others can blanket our spirit, like black silt that slowly filters downward into the hidden recess of our innermost being. The miasma of spiritual darkness sets in.

Is it any wonder we feel so dark inside?

In spite of all I have learned about the power of praise, I still slip into darkness. It's so subtle that it happens even before I'm aware of it.

Recently I took our car to be repaired. The bill was huge! They were supposed to repair the turn signals and the rear lights. I didn't check their work until I got home. One turn signal still didn't work and neither of the rear lights. My son, Bruce, checked them also and said, "Sorry Dad, they don't work."

Why did they tell me it was repaired? This meant I would have to take the car back early the next morning, leave it again for the repairs and find a way home. Why couldn't people do their job right? By that evening one of our children had also done something completely irresponsible and unkind. Why did they do it?

My mind was not at peace. When I went to bed I felt far from peaceful. I couldn't sleep. My entire body was restless. Then it dawned on me what had happened. The blackness was all around me. I was where I didn't belong. People were controlling my emotions, feelings and attitudes.

"Lord, this is all wrong! Please forgive me. My whole purpose is to permit your Holy Spirit to rule in me." As I released the problems to Him, His peace filled my mind. My body relaxed and I drifted off into a sound sleep.

The next morning I took the car back to the garage and patiently told them I needed a little more help. They responded graciously and immediately and began checking the lights.

"Sorry, sir. We can't find anything wrong."

"Nothing wrong?" I looked at the lights myself and sure enough, everything was perfect. Months later they still work perfectly.

Weird? A strange coincidence? What happened, I don't know. The important thing was that I learned one valuable lesson on the importance of staying out of dark places ... of "walking in the light."

I was drawn back into the reality of the moment as we left Stonehenge. But the lesson God had given me in exchange for my disappointment — man's need for this deep inner change — stayed with me.

***

When men listen, God will use them even to change history. Driving across the English countryside reminded us of one man who listened to God. He had been a student at Oxford, not far from Stonehenge, in the first half of the eighteenth century. His name was John Wesley. Many historians tell us that before Wesley came on the scene, England was headed for a revolution similar to the one that rocked France. His message to the rich and poor caused dramatic changes in all aspects of English life. John Wesley and his followers literally begged for pennies to feed the poor. In the process, he spoke so powerfully against sins of all kinds and announced the forgiveness that Christ offers so convincingly that there was a moral revolution. Men from all walks of life came to hear Wesley. Some came to scoff. They left proclaiming the message God gave through this five-feet, four-inch, 110-pound giant.

God is still changing lives. Still speaking to those who will listen. Still releasing His power to those who believe Him.

If your life is in a state of turmoil, maybe God would speak to you about change. But maybe you can't quite hear what He's saying, for that still, small voice can only be heard in the quietness of spirit.

What in your life keeps you from tuning into that still, small voice? Have you been momentarily caught off guard?

God does not author confusion, but the enemy of our souls does. That enemy stalks around like a "roaring lion, seeking whom he may devour." If the roar of circumstances is drowning out God's small, still voice and His peace eludes you, take time to examine some of the tactics the enemy cunningly uses to keep you running in circles and going nowhere.

V

TO KNOW ONE'S ENEMY
... IS TO WIN A THOUSAND BATTLES

Confusion races like wildfire in dry grass, if we give it opportunity. Evil reaches out to control every tongue and every ear it can. As I would not eat from my neighbor's garbage can, I will not listen to the idle chatter of those who pass on malicious information they have heard from others. If the news, however, is good, uplifting, encouraging or edifying, my spirit gladly receives it.

Satan subtly uses anyone who is not alert to his tactics. He even enlists Christians to play major and minor parts in his drama of confusion.

He would love to give us star billing!

He will play to small groups, but he really likes a "full house." And magnanimously lets us take all the credit for the success of his productions.

Confusion surrounds us about everyone and everything. If we permit Satan, he will give us ugly thoughts about people we live with, those we work with and even those we worship with. He uses confusion to destroy homes and churches. Division and strife are two of his favorite weapons.

He convinced Adam and Eve that God hadn't given them the whole truth when He told them not to eat the forbidden fruit. Eating this fruit would give them knowledge of all good and evil. Satan failed to mention that they already knew everything about good. It was only evil they would learn about. And sadly enough for all of us, they learned.

Satan used confusion to create disharmony among Jesus' disciples. As always, he used some seed of truth or goodness and mixed it with innuendo to create strife. He prodded them to debate the issue of who would be greatest in the Kingdom of Heaven.

Satan then strove to unite the disciples against Jesus. Since they loved Jesus, they would "watch over him." When He made the decision to go to Bethany, they took a vote and decided He made the wrong decision. He should not go. Imagine! Twelve men who had seen Jesus do mighty miracles became convinced they knew more about what Jesus should do than Jesus Himself.

If Satan could do that, is it any surprise that he could bring confusion and strife to us?

Perhaps the epitome of confusion was when Satan tried to convince Jesus' family that He was insane. When this failed, the next step was to suggest to people that Jesus was evil. This belief increased in the hearts of men, until they nailed Him to the cross!

Isn't it ironic and fitting, that the very weapon Satan used turned on him and was instrumental in bringing about his eternal defeat? The Bible tells us that if Satan had known God's eternal plan, he would never have crucified the Lord of Glory.(I Cor. 2:8)

Now he knows that his time is short and he uses this weapon of strife at every opportunity to discredit and harm those who are heirs to eternal life. He uses all his cunning to convince humans they should fight against one another.

In my own ministry I have had a man say, "I cannot in good conscience support your work, Merlin. A brother whom I respect has shared something very unfavorable about your past."

"Has he talked with me about it?"

"I don't know about that, but I'm sure he wouldn't say it unless he was sure it was true."

I contacted this individual and said, "I've been told you feel you know something very unfavorable about me and are advising people not to support my ministry. Is this true?"

"Yes, it is," he replied in honesty.

"What is this information and where did you get it?"

"From ... well, I can't give you their name." And so on and on the ever-widening circle of evil gossip grows, inevitably veiled in anonymity.

My case is no different from that of any person who is before the public eye. Satan loves to encourage people to spread gossip about public figures whether they be in the religious, political, entertainment or economic field. Entire careers have been ruined by ...

"I heard from someone who heard from ... "

These things are nearly impossible to trace back to their origin, and they are equally impossible to stop from spreading. In my experience, people who gossip about my life have never once been able to say, "I know this to be fact because I was there, or I talked to someone who was."

The point is this: For two thousand years, Satan has manipulated Christians to turn against one another. It is one of his most effective tools. His whole purpose is to destroy our faith. But if we are wise to his tactics, he need never invade our minds.

Satan is the master of deceit. He thrives on making other people think evil of us. He delights to have us think evil of others. Since God rejoices when others bless you, Satan rejoices when others curse you.

If there are no real grounds for anyone to be against you, Satan will manufacture some. So don't be upset when you learn that someone believes ill of you, when it isn't true. Just purpose in your heart to never believe an ill report *unless* you have positive evidence. And when you do have evidence, claim God's restoration and forgiveness for them, and believe He will do it. Then think of something you can do to be a blessing to that person. This is what Jesus did for us.

Never will I forget the judge before whom I stood in 1945. He had all the evidence against me. I was guilty and admitted it. I had no attorney because I couldn't afford one. The mercy of the court was all I could hope for, and this prospect didn't look too good. But mercy I did receive. Instead of being sentenced to five years in prison I was given five years' probation.

In spite of this I went on to commit further offenses. But over and over God's grace came to me. He even reached into the heart of President Harry S. Truman and inspired him to give me a Presidential pardon. The President had never seen me. By some means he received my war record and decided the old me had to be a new man.

His pardon completely erased my past record. It wasn't until twenty-four years later that I fully realized the significance of the pardon. On all my official records, I could have honestly answered, "No criminal record." There was no record. It was all eliminated by the President. In fact, if I said I *had* a criminal record, I would not have been telling the truth!

God has given us the authority to pardon others. To wipe the slate clean! We may not be able to wipe the offense from their minds, but we *can* wipe it from our own. We can declare the person "PARDONED". The record of the offense against them is *gone*. It no longer hurts us. God can also use our forgiveness to help them. As Stephen was being stoned to death he said, "Father, forgive them." Paul saw and heard. What power was released by Stephen's confession! Millions of lives were eternally changed because Stephen forgave.

I've never had the joy of forgiving a man who went on to be as effective as Paul. But I did have the joy of seeing forgiveness change a man.

A commanding officer once said about me, "The only thing I have against Carothers is that he doesn't take orders very well." He was speaking at the time to my senior chaplain, alluding to my unwillingness to compromise regarding moral principles. But all my senior chaplain heard was "Carothers doesn't take orders very well." In the military this is about as damning a thing as could ever be said about you.

At this point, the chaplain left my commander's office and went back to his own office. He immediately put in a phone call to Washington. In a matter of hours, written orders were on their way transferring me to an overseas station, a "hardship zone," requiring me to be away from my family for a *whole year!*

When the orders arrived, I started making inquiries since my time for overseas duty was still a few months away. Then I learned what the commander was supposed to have said and what the senior chaplain had heard ... and done.

When I confronted my commander, he was shocked and angry, "He misunderstood what I said. I've given you maximum efficiency ratings for all the time you've been here. But I said the wrong words to the wrong person."

Instead of getting angry, I found myself filled with peace. The commander couldn't understand my reaction.

"You should be *fiff#!%⅛ mad!" he shouted.

"No, I should be at peace."

"Well, I wouldn't be. Your overseas orders can't be changed now, no matter what I do."

"But I've already received higher orders, Sir. I was told by my 'Supreme Commander' to always be filled with peace."

The commander said, "Chaplain, you've tried to get through to me before, but I was too hard a nut. This gets to me. Please tell me about this faith thing you've been preaching."

And he went on to receive this "faith thing" ... Jesus.

VI

BATTLE STATIONS!

Satan has lost the war, but he still tries to win every battle he can. When small artillery fails, he brings out the big guns!

One big gun in his arsenal of deception is very effectively camouflaged as "wisdom". The only way we can see through the camouflage is to recognize his tactics for what they are. The Lord has given me some insights about this which may help you to be victorious as you seek to have more of His power in your life.

Our most common source of suffering is what other people do to us. So it stands to reason that other people's source of suffering may be what *we do to them*. Jesus was most explicit in His declaration. He commanded that we love one another. Yet, Satan, by his clever tactics, causes Christians to hurt one another — not only over and over, but nearly continually!

As the Holy Spirit kept impressing on me that Christians are continually hurting each other, as well as those who might become Christians if they weren't continually being hurt, I longed to know more explicitly what He meant.

In my lifetime, while participating in four wars, I have seen ample evidence of man's inhumanity to man. That's pretty much out in the open. But I knew He was wanting to teach me something new ... something so subtle I hadn't even realized it was an enemy.

I knew that people hurt one another with fists, knives and bullets, not to mention reckless driving which kills about 50,000 people a year! But there was a less obvious weapon involved here. The Spirit was emphasizing within me the pain which we inflict upon each other every day, but without bloodshed. And these invisible wounds are inflicted in the name of "goodness".

This is very like Satan. Being the author of deception, his methods are so clever that only the Holy Spirit can enable us to catch him in the act.

If you don't "punch people out", take out after them with knives and guns, or deliberately run them off the freeway, what could you do that hurts them? Might it be ... criticism!

It began long ago.

Satan criticized God. He quietly suggested God was doing wrong. Then he spread this innuendo throughout all Heaven until other angels rebelled against God. He told man the same thing, "God is unfair. He just isn't treating you right."

Man learned to criticize quickly. Adam blamed Eve. Eve blamed Satan. So the destructive chain continued down through history and so it continues today.

Satan's goals were clear. He knew how to prepare man's mind for the ultimate goal. *Get God's creation to criticize Him.*

We know that a radio does not create sound. It receives what is transmitted through the air. Satan, being the "prince of the power of the air" can bombard our minds with critical thoughts! Of course, he is very deceptive in his strategies. He will get us to accept these critical thoughts, until eventually we think they originated with us and soon they become our very own. So much so that we begin to treasure them as "intuitive wisdom".

The mind decides, "I believe I have the gift of discernment. Now I will know what is wrong with people. I can be a blessing to others by revealing their weak areas . . . so they can be better."

How cleverly we become ensnared.

This critical spirit makes even more insidious inroads.

Someone unexpectedly gives us a gift. A mind trained in the art of criticism immediately responds, "Why did he give this to me? He must want something." Or, "His conscience must be bothering him about something."

Their good gift has been perverted by the wisdom from below.

But if we receive no gift, the critical mind reacts, "If he wasn't so selfish he might give me something once in a while."

The spirit of criticism can never be fed enough. It will search high and low to nurse its malignant grievances and grasp hold on the most innocent actions of others.

Has anyone ever passed you on the street without looking at you and the thought flashed across your mind, "He deliberately avoided me!" It is more likely that he was so preoccupied he would pass his own mother unnoticed, his heart burdened by a million cares you know *nothing* about.

But Satan isn't interested in encouraging us to show grace to our brothers. He wants us to pile a crushing weight of criticism on top of the burden others may already be carrying.

The critical spirit always tries to second guess the other person. "He said 'this', but he really meant 'that'. He says one thing to me, but he probably says something else to others."

What a heavy burden judging is!

There is a certain element of pride in judging. We're so sure "we know". And knowledge puffs us up.

John learned the painful way that "pride goeth before destruction". His pride destroyed his trust in a valued friend, and, in a sense it diminished his own integrity.

John and his friend had started a business from practically nothing. Years of toil had developed a company they were both proud of. Income was increasing on a steady basis. They were providing a much needed service to the community. They certainly enjoyed working together and were the best of friends in every sense of the word.

But, one day, John began to notice his partner was acting strangely. He noticed his friend poring over the account books, and he somehow seemed less open than he had been. John observed him speaking secretively to the executives under them. At times, when John entered the room, he became aware that his friend lowered his voice on the phone. The more he saw, the more obvious it became. His friend was plotting to take over the business!

John endured agony. His health suffered. His disposition changed at work and at home. Criticism of his friend grew inside of him.

Finally, his friend came into his office one day and said,"John, I have to talk to you. We have been friends for a long time and this is something I hate to have to tell you."

"Here it comes," thought John. "He's finally coming out in the open with his rotten scheming."

"The doctor has told me I probably have only a few months left to live. I've been working hard trying to get my end of the business straightened out for you. I'm making some progress, but my strength is slipping."

***

Here was a man literally giving his life for his friend and yet being suspected of selfish motives. John suffered the agony of suspicion which was much more harmful to him than if his friend had actually planned to, and had succeeded in taking over the business. Companies can be rebuilt in time. Money can be earned in many ways. But destruction of our own health and spirit is far more difficult to restore.

The critical spirit grows inside of us with very little encouragement. While admirable qualities need to be carefully nurtured in order to survive, criticism flourishes like scraggly weeds!

Showing no favorites, it attacks the rich and poor alike; the young and the old; the educated and the unread. It attacks anyone who is wise in his own estimate. It weaves its tangled web of suspicion into homes, offices, churches — wherever people are.

Until we realize what is going on, we are unprepared to do anything about it. Criticism does however, follow a predictable pattern.

First, think frequently about obviously evil things such as Hitler, Stalin, murder, crime and world conflict. There is perhaps nothing you can do about these things, but you can at least meditate on the horrible and evil conditions that have been and are in the world. Criticism begins to take root.

Next, become proficient in observing the weaknesses and mistakes of others around you. We can pride ourselves in being able to perceive when others are lying, being selfish, being worldly and unspiritual, or being unfaithful. Because after all, we do have the gift of discernment ... don't we?

Eventually, almost unawares, we have fallen into the trap of fabricating evil in others to satisfy the appetite of the critical spirit now firmly entrenched within.

Finally, we are exhibiting full-blown symptoms of the "But Syndrome."

"We have wonderful people in our church,'but' some of them are lazy."

It's true there are lazy people in any group. Must we, however, attach that thought to the beauty of the church Jesus died for? Why not let others hear a positive report: "We have wonderful people in our church. Some of the most enthusiastic, loving, interesting people you would ever want to meet."

"My wife is one of the best in the world,but at times she irritates me beyond belief!" Of course your wife has her idiosyncrasies. Must the world be told? It certainly takes no wisdom to see that people irritate one another. On the other hand, to say that you have a really great husband or wife — that's news! In fact, we may hear it so seldom, it fits into the category of rare news!

"My children are a real blessing, but at times they drive me crazy." The ones who are really being driven crazy are other parents who have *real* problem children but who now have to listen to us complain!

"I have a fine pastor, but he never comes to see me."

When this was said to me once, I recommended that they go out of their way to make their pastor feel welcome in their home. I suggested that the wife cook some of her favorite dishes and shower the pastor with her culinary art. They took the advice and in a few months were filled with praise for what a great pastor they had. They killed their own criticism by acts of kindness.

***

It is not a big step from imagining evil in our fellow human beings to criticizing God. Satan uses our lack of understanding to draw us into this final trap. He knows that some of God's ways are completely incomprehensible to us, so he bombards our minds with the thought, "God, I think you are wrong about this. You should do it this way."

Our minds become conditioned to actually think it's okay to give God advice, as if the Creator of the universe needed our advice on anything!

What we need is His advice, such as ... "trust in the Lord with all your heart and lean not to your own understanding." (Prov. 3:5, 6) "In everything give thanks, for this is the will of God for you in Christ Jesus." (I Thess. 5:18)

When we do not seek His counsel first, we begin to lean on our own reasoning. And we begin to slide into impatience, anxiety and doubt.

We are no longer willing to persevere by praising Him in all things because, after all, shouldn't He have taken care of this problem yesterday? Yes, we will answer back to

God, after having been carefully and oh so subtly conditioned to see what is wrong with everyone and everything around us. Besides, we have a "better idea".

We don't want to hear God speak to us and say, "Who are you, a mere man, to criticize and contradict and answer back to God? Will what is formed say to Him that formed it, why have you made me thus?" (Romans 9:20).

But we do criticize Him when we say, "Why did you let this happen to me, God? Why aren't you doing something about things now? ... "

He only answers, "Trust Me. I am working out what is the very best for you. Don't run ahead of My timetable."

Jesus' life was always on schedule with God's timetable. Although He had ample opportunity, He never permitted the spirit of criticism to find a place in Him. Though He suffered through humiliation that should have evoked scathing criticism from Him, His response was always, "Father, forgive them."

When others said, "Stone her to death," He said, "I do not condemn you. Go and sin no more."

When Judas was about to betray Jesus, He said, "What you must do, do quickly."

When his disciples reported to Him what others were doing, He said, "What is that to you? Follow Me."

When they wanted to call down fire from heaven, He said, "You know not what spirit you speak from. I have not come to destroy."

Jesus could look on evil and see it for what it was. He knew its source. Never did he turn His back on evil or ignore it. But when the time came to do something about it, He did what needed to be done. The real enemy was evil, not the people it used. And Jesus always got right to the core of the problem, whereas you and I focus only on its outer surface.

Because His judgement was based on perfect wisdom, unburdened by supposition and false accusations, Jesus could say to people, "You've broken God's law. But I love you and want to forgive you."

Whereas criticism found no place in Him, it does quite easily in you and me. Criticism can destroy even the most sacred of human relationships — marriage. A husband assumes his wife is angry, when actually the wife feels ill.

A wife presumes her husband is stingy, when in reality he is burdened with worry about where the next house payment is coming from! Unwilling to admit that he is afraid, he responds angrily.

A wife fears losing her husband, but reacts in a way that convinces him he is no longer wanted.

We are continually confusing evil with our own clouded perceptions — reading evil into good. We let the seeds of criticism become so rooted in our natures that we can't discern when we are really seeing evil or when we are just falsely accusing others.

The power of Christ will flow in us more freely as we learn the beautiful art of looking at others and not seeing reasons to be critical. This requires changes in *us, not in them.*

VII

VICTORY OVER CRITICISM

Are you pained when people find fault with you? Can someone ruin a perfectly beautiful day by picking on you?

Do you have a fault that others keep pointing out? Does it hurt you? Others may never be willing or able to ignore your faults, because they are human, too. Still, we ought to be comforted by the thought that usually only our obvious faults will be seen by others. It is the less obvious things that should concern us.

The most subtle and insidious problem is our *potential* for evil. In our natural state, each of us has at some time and in some way rebelled against God. Each of us still has this potential. We, like Satan, could rise up against God.

"Oh, not I," we might speedily react. "I would never dare rebel against God."

That is because we *know* how powerless we are. But what if we learned more about power? What if we learned how to move mountains, and how to control people? How far could we go in knowledge and pride before we would want to "be like God?"

"To be god of your own life" ... this is exactly what Satan offers many people today, subtly disguised in the form of mind-control, do-it-yourself-type religions and false methods of "acquiring all knowledge." The first lie Satan used to deceive Adam and Eve was that they could know as much as God.

The human capacity to control and dominate the lives and minds of others has already been demonstrated. Its tragic consequences have been dramatically illustrated in the fatal episode of Jonestown. And again by Khomeini of Iran.

God knows what we are capable of. And so He has to apply His grace to give us any rights or benefits at all.

As Christians we still have within us the evil potential to destroy ourselves and others. History contains plentiful illustrations of how cruel Christians have been when they thought they were acting in Jesus' name. We must admit that, even though we strive to be Christlike, we often fail miserably to be like Him.

By His grace, I am learning to be thankful when I am accused of doing or being wrong. Part of me thinks, "It would be great to be well-thought of by all men." But then I'm quickly reminded of Jesus' words, "Woe unto you when all men speak well of you ... so did they to the false prophets." (Luke 6:26)

Paul's life was an example of God's grace and forgiveness. Others had plenty to criticize him for. He persecuted the church severely before God stopped him in his tracks on the road to Damascus. Then the Lord used him so mightily that He allowed him a "thorn in the flesh" to keep him from being lifted up in pride.

Knowing the destructive power of pride and self-righteousness, God permits us to feel the sting of the criticism by others.

45

Realizing how easy it is to grow in pride, and knowing how displeasing this is to God, I'm learning to say, "Thank you, God, for the past and present. Let others point out my failures as frequently as I need to be reminded of them, but let their criticism cause me to love You more and to be increasingly grateful for your grace. If you gave me what I deserved, I could never hope for eternal life. I couldn't even enjoy this life. But you have made me the happiest man in the world. I will be forever grateful."

Think of the new joy we will have when we can receive criticism and not feel offended. His peace will replace the anger and ugly resentment we once felt. Whatever others say, or feel, or do will now work for us, instead of against us. His power is being released in us.

We can trust Him to keep His promise to make all things work together for our good . . . just as He did for the man who worked for a prosperous company that had lost a large sum of money.

Searching through computer records, even the experts became bogged down in confusion. Checking back and forth between accounts payable and receivable, and property inventories, they found huge discrepancies but couldn't determine where the money had gone. It was evident that someone had perfected a scheme to siphon off company resources.

Someone had to be blamed. A rumor began circulating that a "certain vice president" was responsible. The man was furious. He demanded that his name be cleared. But because the center of attention was now focused on him, the newspapers featured him as a prime suspect!

No evidence was ever found that this man was guilty, but because of the adverse publicity he was fired.

Humiliated and crushed, he believed his life was ruined. His family too, suffered humiliation. They sold everything and moved to another part of the country.

A new next door neighbor gave this family a copy of *Prison to Praise*. Not being in the habit of reading Christian books, they were a little annoyed. Then one of the daughters read it and decided to attend church with the neighbors. There she accepted Christ. She prevailed on her father to read *Prison to Praise*, and then convinced him to go to church with her. He, too, received Christ!

This man soon established himself in a new business with another company and was doing well until word got around that he had been fired from his last job for stealing company funds. His first reaction was to be hurt, resentful and angry. But he quietly expressed his innocence and left it up to the new company to do as they wished. Meanwhile he did even more. He put praise to practice. He thanked God for using his past misfortune to work a miracle in his family. They were all coming to know Christ and were growing in the Spirit. God had used the past to strengthen them in the present.

This man is now a dynamic witness for Christ. His company and community have come to appreciate him as a man of integrity.

He regularly leads others to Christ. He still encounters the occasional sly remark which implies, "What did you do with all that money?" And of course, this hurts. But he sees the hand of God working for good in all of his life.

***

An army officer was dismissed from the service under charges of misappropriation of government funds. He was so bitter over being treated unfairly that his health rapidly deteriorated. He became so unfit to live with that his wife and children left him. Everything he had was gradually lost and he was crushed by the circumstances of his life. One day he decided to end it all. He committed suicide. What a tragic waste! If only he had let God make his problem work for him.

Our problems may be physical, mental or spiritual. People tend to aggravate our problems by their critical attitudes towards us. They may think they are trying to help us. Their motives may be clothed in spirituality, "Let us pray for Mrs. Smith. Some unconfessed sin may be why she has such problems." Now, who could condemn anyone for asking others to pray?

But we should not be upset. Instead, we can make these sly attacks work *for* us. God will be pleased if He sees by our smile that we are claiming His protection. He knows far worse things about us that He doesn't allow Satan to broadcast. In fact, we can often be grateful for the lies that are told about us, because the truth would be so much worse.

God will accept our trust in Him and He will be our defense. Our own peace of mind will grow instead of being shattered by things other people think or don't think. His power is working.

Jesus was and is God and He often came under attack. Now you and I are guilty of many things. (And capable of many more!) But they accused Him of things he had *not* done. And they killed Him. So don't be surprised when we are unjustly criticized.

If our witness is effective for God, Satan will be marshalling his forces against us. We should not be surprised when Satan uses the lies of others, twisting the truth, to attack us.

To be a Christian means to expect to receive the same kind of treatment Jesus did. He told us that a servant is not greater than his master and if they persecuted Him they would persecute us.

Our defense against criticism should be to respond according to God's instructions. In Romans 12:14-21 we are told to pray for those who persecute us and ask God to bless them! To overcome evil with good.

Anyone can repay with evil those who persecute them. But it takes the Spirit of Christ in a man to respond by going up when others are putting him down. I see it like a see-saw with me on one end and Jesus on the other. If I permit troubles to rest on my shoulders I am pressed down. If I permit my troubles to be on His shoulders, where he told me to place them, then my troubles are pushing me up!

What I'm teaching is not mere theory. It is living reality. As we respond as Jesus did, He will work in us. For that same Spirit that raised Him from the dead will also enable us to live as He did.

In fulfillment of His promise, He will be a well of joy springing up in us. The joy of the Lord is strength that enables us to stand. When I'm attacked, I'm tempted to be down in the mouth about it. Then I realize what is happening, and I look up to Him in praise.

To help me more clearly understand *why* this works, the Spirit gave me a vision of a man being stoned . . .

When the first stone hit him, I could see that it hurt. He said, "Praise the Lord." But his words really seemed to be saying, "Lord, I can't do anything to stop them so I will just praise you."

The second stone hit harder and he seemed to suffer even more. But he persisted in praising God. In the vision, I knew he was thinking, "I still don't know why You are permitting this, but I will trust You."

As the third stone struck, it became apparent that he felt no pain. His faith rose. Now he praised the Lord with enthusiasm.

The fourth stone fell short and missed him.

The fifth stone paused in mid-air. The man continued his praise to God. The stone reversed its course!

This is praise that has power. It takes what is evil and makes it work for our good. God has placed this power in our hands, and we must use it — not just think about it — but engage our wills to take action.

Behind the scenes, God will take that weapon which was meant for our detriment and turn it into a blessing in disguise. We have His Word. "No weapon formed against you shall prosper." (Isa. 54:17)

Our praises to God are the energizing force which turns the tables on Satan, causing him to beat a hasty retreat! This is because God inhabits our praises and Satan cannot remain in the presence of praise. "Resist the devil and he will flee from you." (James 4:7)

If you've ever thought of praise as passive acceptance of everything that happens, you have lost sight of one of the most active, positive forces in the world. God would never have directed us so emphatically to praise Him if He had not known how powerfully it would work for our good!

Learning to rejoice in our infirmities or the reproaches others load on us is a little like enjoying a beautiful rose. Roses, of course, have thorns. The secret is to learn to enjoy the roses, even though faced with the possibility of getting stuck with a thorn.

What did Paul do with his "thorn in the flesh"? He learned to rejoice in his infirmities and reproaches, for the grace of God rested more mightily on him!

Praise releases new strength in our physical being and fortifies us against every device Satan uses. As we put more praise power into our lives, criticism will shrivel up and be swept away like the dead leaves of winter. New life will blossom in our souls, like the flowers of spring heralding newness of life in the wake of winter's bleakness.

The evidence clearly indicates that criticism must go! This is not to say we retreat to an ivory tower and don rose-colored glasses.

We can look at things for what they are, but we can choose to respond to them in a way that will not allow them to make destructive inroads into our own spirit through the well-trod path of criticism. As we bring every thought captive to Jesus, He will help us, by His Spirit, to meditate on that which is "honest, just, pure, lovely and of good report." (Phil.4:8)

By living in His Spirit, we grow more and more confident regarding that most important moment in all eternity when we will stand before a holy God with nothing to say in our own defense. Powerless in and of ourselves, we will stand in the "power that worketh in us".

We shall see the glorious strength which flows from the One who forgave others and taught us to do the same.

Jesus will approach the Father and present us to Him. And, then and there, God will put to an end the accusations leveled against us who inherit His eternal kingdom.

He will do it by ushering us into the kingdom with a joyous pronouncement: "Well done, thou good and faithful servant ... enter into the joy of thy Lord." (Matt. 25:21)

Now unto Him that is able to ... *present you faultless* before the presence of His glory with exceeding joy ... be glory and majesty, dominion and power, both now and ever." (Jude 24 & 25)

* * *

From that moment on we will never again need to learn how to accept criticism! But for now our assignment is clear. We must learn to respond to criticism as peacefully as Jesus did. As we do, He will *make* it work for our good.

VIII

TO HIM WHO OVERCOMES

Perhaps you know people who are miserable because they expect everything in life to go well. When it doesn't, they are frantic. Perhaps you even know Christians who always expect everything to go smoothly. Then, when trouble comes, they throw up their hands and groan, "I thought God was going to take better care of me!"

I expect life to be difficult at times. It always has been and it always will be. Job 5:7 puts it this way. "Man is born unto trouble, as the sparks fly upward."

The process of birth is not easy. It's tough to live and it's tough to die. So whatever happens that seems to be bad, shouldn't take us by surprise. (And if, perchance, something does happen that's easy to take, if you're like me, you won't have much difficulty putting up with it!)

We should expect Satan to try to create problems for us. That is his business. I am not particularly surprised when people cross my path who are mean, ugly and selfish. The world has many of them. It is only to be expected that I should run across my share.

But I have an even greater expectation from God. I expect God to take perfect care of me when I trust Him (Ps.34:19).

Our Lord was victorious over evil at its worst. He wants to be victorious in us. He told us, "Be of good cheer, for I have overcome the world!" So, no matter what is going on, I know He wants us to be filled with joy. And keep in mind that joy does not depend on our circumstances, but can be ours in spite of circumstances!

If someone punches you in the stomach when you least expect it, it can hurt badly. But if you see it coming and tense your muscles, you can take the blow with a minimum of pain. That means, of course, that those muscles should be strong as a consequence of regular exercise.

So, I'm trying to learn how to keep my spiritual muscles strengthened. I expect trouble to come, but in a positive way, since I know something good will come out of it. When it does come, I'm not caught off guard. And, while we may expect trouble to come, we should also expect our spiritual strength in Christ to continually grow stronger.

Please keep in mind that, although God doesn't cause these experiences to come upon us, He may allow us to go through them because He is going to teach us something and bless us through them. He is going to use it, and make it work for our good (Romans 8:28). He is going to build us up in faith, in patience and in praise. He is going to teach us how to win battles in the spiritual warfare we are engaged in ... to come out the victor!

Paul shared a valuable insight: "When I am weak, then I am strong." He was experiencing Christ's strength in his weakness. This is what Jesus was talking about when He said, "in your weakness is My strength made perfect." This lesson is so important that God allows us many opportunities to learn it.

It is not surprising to learn that Satan would try to hit us with something harder than we could bear. If we had to depend on Satan's being fair about it, we would be defeated from the start! *But God promises* to let nothing touch our lives which would be more than we could bear or that wouldn't be for our good. So I'm depending on Him. This means Satan is defeated from the start.

Today, we are all feeling the effects of the devaluation of the American dollar, although it clearly has "In God We Trust" written on the back of it. But a life which has "In God I Trust" written across it can expect time to increase the value of this investment in trust. And its value goes up the most when times are hardest.

If you have been discouraged because life hasn't been treating you sweetly and kindly, let your thinking be reoriented. Life can be bitter and mean. *But God is the equalizer.* He stands ready to always deliver in time of trouble. "Many are the afflictions of the righteous: *but the Lord* delivereth him out of them." (Ps. 34:19)

Jesus knew trouble was ahead. He tried to prepare the disciples to be strengthened during the time of trouble until the time of deliverance came. He plainly told them what would happen to Him, before it happened. But they couldn't hear Him because they wanted to expect only the best. So they were shattered when the worst came.

There are those who will tell you that if you live right, everything will go great for you. But it isn't always true. Some people who live the best often have the worst things happen to them. Those who work the hardest sometimes have the least.

Don't base life on a foundation which, like the shifting sand, can be washed away when the storms come. Build on the Solid Rock. Know that security is never dependent upon getting "good breaks" or "good treatment". Don't be surprised if you experience the worst from nature, others, or life itself. But at the same time, be expecting victory in Christ!

Expect Him to always be with you, *exactly as He promised*. Expect God to take every sorrow, pain, hard knock, defeat or rejection and work something good out of it for you. (Rom. 8:28) ... His power is at work in all our circumstances. This is our rightful inheritance as God's children.

A woman shared with me a "close encounter of the right kind." She had many experiences of rejection in childhood which kept her from trusting other people. As an adult, she became a Christian and finally began to open up. She began to trust a small group of friends, whom she felt very close to ... to the point where the group became her security. God does not want people to be our security. Therefore, He had to allow her to experience the rejection of "the group". And it hurt. It was shattering.

She went home to her bedroom and shut the door. She wanted to shut the world out. Lying on the bed, curled up in a fetal position, shutting out everything else, the pain of rejection hit hard ... and deeply. Then, suddenly, there in the darkness of her depression, eyes shut tightly, she said it was as if a TV screen had come on in a dark room. There before her vision was a "person" who smiled at her. He said nothing, but His eyes spoke volumes of love ... the most lovely face, eyes shining with great depths of love and acceptance ... "I'm so glad to see you! I like you ... I love you!"

She said at this point, she was so startled by all of this that she opened her eyes ... and it was all over. But the feeling of warmth and love that filled her remained, not only throughout the day, but for several days. Jesus loved her and He was her *best friend*.

Asked to describe how He looked, she found it impossible to say. But she would never forget the eyes ... eyes that communicated the depths and riches of God's love , from which we can't be separated.

She was reminded that Jesus too, was "wounded in the house of His friends." So He knew exactly the pain ... and came, literally, to exchange His love for the pain of rejection.

The Bible tells us that He is our perfect high priest ...

"for we have not an high priest which cannot be touched with the feeling of our infirmities; but was in all points tempted like as we are, yet without sin." (Heb. 4:15)

When we experience pain, He too is touched with the feeling of our pain, for He has been there. But He was victorious over it. He wants to replace our defeat with His victory.

I am trying to share a real fact of life, not merely a philosophical reflection. If you are willing to let God take these words and change any part of you that needs to be changed, He will cause you to be grounded on the foundation that is immovable.

We retain only a small percentage of what we read, so it is important that these words do something for you that will become an actual part of you. In this way, there will be nothing to remember, just a lifetime of living what you will learn as you read this book. So don't wait until you have time to forget these words. Go ahead now and claim your inheritance in Christ. Claim the promise in Romans 8:28.

Purpose in your heart that, from now on, you will not be upset by anything life throws at you. When troubles come, through people or circumstances, you are prepared to be an overcomer. And you are going to win! You have to know this! Jesus promised to never — no never — under any circumstances, leave or forsake us. His overcoming power is available, and He wants to share it with us.

I meet or hear from people daily who would be set free of their burdens readily if they would only claim their inheritance. God has already provided our victory over every mean thing in life. He does not necessarily promise to change the "mean thing", but He has promised to take the "mean things" and make them work for our good if we trust Him. Our faith in this promise grows every time we exercise it. We can only exercise it as we have opportunities. But if we have opportunities and don't use them, we will eventually be in real trouble.

Satan will never take it easy on us just because we have

problems. Nothing is fair about his tactics. He is like a lion which singles out the weakest animal of the herd and heads for it. It isn't fair or honorable for a lion to select the weakest prey, but that is exactly what he does.

Peter knew this was an accurate picture of Satan when he called him a "roaring lion, seeking whom he might devour." Satan always lurks about, looking for our "weak spots."

When we are most tired, the most weary, having the most problems — those are the times when he will pounce on us. No mercy. No fair play. So don't waste your time meditating on the unfairness of it all. But remember, instead, Jesus has promised to be our strength when we are at our weakest. He has proven it over and over again in the lives of countless people just like you and me. Remember, it's His power, not ours. It's not based on our own ability, but on His integrity ... the integrity of His Word!

When you are thrown into the lion's den, don't expect the lions to disappear. They will be right there waiting. They will roar and do their best to paralyze you with fear. Let them roar! But expect them to be powerless over you.

When Daniel was thrown to the lions, he trusted God, and he was not disappointed.

Because of the way Daniel proved the power of his faith, I can almost wish that I had been there to see it work! But God has other ways to show His power working in us.

IX

THE POWER OF EXPECTATIONS

"As a man thinketh in his heart, so is he." This is just as sure as any principle of math or science.

In geometry there are certain known axioms or rules which must be accepted in order to get the correct answer. There are also "rules" that must be applied in order to have God answer our prayers. If we ignore these rules, we cannot get our prayers answered or our problems solved.

These rules are not so ambiguous that we can say we don't understand, or so complicated that we can say, "I can't do it." The only reason we would fail to comply with these simple rules would be our refusal to do so.

Sounds ridiculous, doesn't it? Why would anyone refuse to do what he could, if by so doing it would cause God to answer his prayer?

Like some, you may have decided to experiment with prayer by trying to believe God would answer some "way-out" prayer, just to see if He would.

You look at a mountain, close your eyes and pray, "When I open my eyes, God, I believe You will have removed the mountain." When you open your eyes, what so you see?

I used to try to create a powder-blue Buick convertible out of my faith. I had carefully read and reread the Scriptural promises regarding asking and receiving. It seemed quite clear to me that the Bible said, "Ask and you will receive." In a vague sort of way I understood that I had to believe before God would give to me. I understood the asking part but not the believing part.

Frequently I would close my eyes and strain to believe that when I opened them, there the Buick convertible would be. I was willing to practice and practice until my dream came true. But, my faith began to subside when after countless efforts my powder-blue Buick convertible didn't appear. Was God angry with me for praying such a silly prayer? No, I know he wasn't. Rather, I believe He was smiling at me and saying, "Merlin, you will understand My promises later." But, frankly, I was more interested in what I wanted.

And now, just recently, and thirty five years later, God has revealed to me why my prayers were not answered. My brother telephoned me from Pennsylvania and said, "Merlin, how would you like to have a brand new Cadillac convertible?"

I said, "Bert, they don't make Cadillac convertibles any more. They made the last ones in 1976."

"I'm still asking you, Merlin, how would you like a brand new Cadillac convertible?"

So I said, "I don't know what you mean but I sure would love to have a convertible. I've wanted one all my life."

"Well, I have one for you if you want to fly here and pick it up. It's brand new, has never been driven, and has been in a warm, dry garage since 1976."

To say the least, I was speechless. Finally I was able to ask, "What kind of a Cadillac is it?"

It took Bert a few minutes to tell me that it was the luxury Eldorado with everything that General Motors had ever put on a car — power everything — and on and on.

"But how did you get it, Bert?"

"My boss died recently and left several brand new cars in his garage. He had bought models that were the last of their kind, knowing they would rise in value if he kept them a few years. His son offered me the choice of any car I wanted. I selected the special edition Lincoln and then said, 'My brother in California sure could use that convertible.' He surprised me by saying, 'He can have it at one fourth its value if you want him to have it'."

Mary and I flew back to Pennsylvania. When I walked into the garage and saw the gleaming, shiny, new Cadillac convertible something very special happened to me. It was as if time stood still and I heard God's voice echoing to me from way off, "Merlin, now that you have learned to not ask me for such silly things, I can give them to you." I stood there with tears running down my face and I'm sure looking very blessed. Even as I write this there are tears in my eyes as I again realize how good God is to us. He always hears us! He always wants to supply our needs and even what we want. But, there are so many things we need to learn and so many important changes that need to be made in us before He will answer all our prayers.

As I'm driving through town here in Escondido, California and make a stop, people often say, "That's the most beautiful car I've ever seen!" I sometimes imagine that people who know me are thinking, "There goes Carothers in his flashy car. He must be terribly wealthy to own such a car." Then I smile to myself and think, "If they only knew how rich my Father is and how much He wants to bless us when we learn to trust Him."

We Christians often pray for things to come at the wrong time and for the wrong reasons. It doesn't work, and yet we keep on trying.

Jesus told us that correct prayer *always* works. It is always answered. All we have to do is learn now to pray rightly! Why not practice?

Look at the "mountain", close your eyes and pray, "God, when I open my eyes, I believe that mountain will be exactly where you want it to be!"

Open your eyes and where do you think it will be? You are right! Exactly where it was. And you believed it would be there. Your prayer fitted your expectation.

Then pray, "Lord, I believe that You have that 'mountain' (your problem) there for a purpose. I am going to thank you for its being exactly where it is. I will even be glad its there." Then practice being glad the mountain is there.

You can extend your expectations until you cease to resent the "mountain" presence in your life. God is responding to your faith and it is growing. The mountain can come alive with new meaning for you, for the first time in your life.

Then the day comes when you need to get on the other side of that "mountain". It would be easy to say, "Lord, remove it so I can get past it quickly." But if you couldn't believe God would do it, ask Him to do what you can believe He will do.

"Lord, I've come to enjoy your mountain, and now I'm going to enjoy walking right over it. I believe You will give me strength and help me rejoice every step of the way, regardless of how difficult the journey may be."

Your expectations can be equal to your prayers.

As you travel over the mountain, there will probably be ample opportunities to complain over hardships. Your feet may hurt. Your body may get tired. But that would not be the time to give up. God helped you to be glad *for* the mountain and helped you to enjoy beginning your climb upward. Now, *believe* He will help you get over the top! He hasn't failed you yet, so why not believe Him? Could it be that He will give you renewed and greater faith as you make your way to the top — not to speak of patience and perseverance? Yes, He will. For He has promised to supply all your needs.

Picture what will happen when you reach the top. God answered your expectations. Your view is breathtaking. Things surely look different from the top of the mountain!

Everything in you is now glad you came — glad you climbed that mountain! You have believed God each step of your journey, and for you, the mountain has been removed.

Imagine facing one thousand mountains and always reaching the same conclusion. "God is with me. He always gets me over each mountain just as He promised."

Then comes the day when you are physically unable to climb a mountain. You can't walk up by yourself. But you have learned much.

You now know how God has responded to your every need. You know He will remove this mountain for you. When you close your eyes to pray, you expect it to be gone when you open your eyes, or that God will provide some extraordinary means to get you across. You are so in tune with God that you know He couldn't fail to meet your needs.

This is the kind of faith that makes prayer work. It always works! It has never failed.

Many, many people have cried out to God to remove mountains *before* they have learned to believe Him. But in climbing your mountains you have been learning to believe Him.

Learning to believe is not something we have to go to school to acquire. Nor do we have to go into a secluded monastery to learn the secrets of prayer.

The answers are hidden in the problems. All we have to do is to start with the mountain (problem) God has provided us. It is there for a reason. Take a new look at it. See it as God's special gift to teach you something important.

Of course, the human part of us says, "If He had only left out the mountain — my problem — I wouldn't have to learn how to get across it in the first place."

Yes, this is true. But God knows how much we need to learn to deal with mountains, so He provides these opportunities.

What is your opportunity? What mountains are you facing? Children growing up in a turbulent and permissive society? Husband or wife threatening to leave you? The possible loss of your ability to earn a living? Loss of health? Any one of these is a mountainous opportunity, but we need to see it for what it is before we can begin to pray the prayer that God can answer.

God sees life for His children as having perfect purpose and design. He wrote the script, so to speak. Whatever is, is coming from His will. Think of your life as that of a character in a TV drama. What will happen as the plot develops? You don't know. The man operating the TV station doesn't know. Who controls what happens? The scriptwriter. We may not like his plot or conclusion, but we can't deny that he controls it.

God says that He knows the end from the beginning. He says He will make the end be for our good if we will believe and trust Him.

A scriptwriter doesn't have to worry about supplying automobiles, hotels, airplanes or props for the show. He just writes the script. But God not only writes the story, He supplies all the props. He knows where everything goes, and why. He asks only that we trust Him.

We may have to crawl all the way up the mountain on hands and knees, covered with cuts and bruises. We may hate every foot of our journey, but that is up to us. We might turn back a thousand times and declare we aren't interested in getting to the other side.

We may even rebel and say, "I'm not going another step of the way!"

Why not scale the heights with joy and praise? This is how praise helps us to keep in step with God's plan. We learn that He is in control and that He is providing *all* our needs. Whatever is needed to climb that mountain!

When we are trying to cross our mountain, and make a wrong turn that leads us into a deadend ravine, what does it mean? Where is God?

He is right there, waiting for us to realize we took a wrong turn. Our being angry or frustrated will not help our situation one bit. But if we are filled with joy that God is using our mistakes for our good, great things will begin happening. His power will be released to make it so.

I know a young man who took a plane trip to a country on the other side of the world. There he transferred to a smaller plane that looked so decrepit, he kicked the tires to see if they would go flat!

When he got on the plane, he discovered the foreign pilot was drunk. There was no co-pilot. After a shaky take-off, it started to rain.

The plane bounced all over the skies and seemed doomed to crash into the mountains below! The young man kept wondering why God had brought him to the other side of the world to die in such a ridiculous way. He was the only passenger in this 40-passenger plane, plus one steward. He prayed fervently while he and the steward clung to their seats.

As he prayed, he realized the steward was not a Christian. So he began sharing the plan of salvation with him. The steward was so frightened that he immediately responded and received Christ as his Savior. He went on to become a faithful servant of God in a country that has few active Christians.

Did God arrange for one young man to fly half-way around the world and face death in that decrepit airplane, flown by a drunken pilot, just to lead that one steward to Christ?

He did. God will do anything to help men and women receive His Son. Because you and I are His servants, He has a perfect right to direct our paths into airplanes, hospitals, prisons or courts — wherever He can use our witness. All we need to do is to learn to trust Him . . . and to be obedient.

We may seldom see the eventual results of where He leads us. But that is not important. The important issue for each Christian to settle is that, when God provides a mountain or a valley of any kind, it is to bless us and build His kingdom. The more we rejoice in this reality, the more He is able to increase our faith.

By and by we can look at a mountain with full assurance of God's participation with us. When we say, "Move," it moves! Anything as spectacular as this can be written into the script only when we have a close personal relationship with the Author!

The Author could dictate, "And when Mr. Believit spoke, the mountain moved." That event immediately becomes a factual part of the story.

To create the story with the author, we must be of one spirit with Him. If we are of one mind, and the author is of another, whatever we say is likely to differ from what He says. But when we are united with Him, so that our thoughts become His thoughts, the mountains we feel led to speak to will move because it is His purpose as well. We are then living by the faith of the Son of God — His very faith.

All over the world, people are learning how to be one with the Father. They all agree that it isn't easy to rejoice in all that God allows. But they also agree that as soon as they learn to trust Him in one thing, it is easier to trust Him in two.

Zero in on whatever problem you are having in your life now, and believe God has it there for a reason. Rejoice in it. Then rejoice some more. Keep rejoicing, until you are able to really know your situation is a part of God's plan. I would hesitate to tell you to do this if I had not seen with my own eyes and heard with my ears the exciting results!

I once knew a man who was scheduled to have one of his legs amputated. Every fiber of his mind and body rebelled. He had excelled in many kinds of sports. Losing a leg was like losing his life. In fact, he seriously considered ending his life. He faced a mountain that to him was insurmountable.

He prayed for God to heal the leg. But he wasn't ready for a prayer like that. And he couldn't visualize God using a horrible thing like the loss of a leg for any good. His prayers went unanswered.

After the operation, he was silently morose and very bitter. Then someone gave him a praise book. As he read it, he began to believe that God was working in his life. He saw God using the tragedy to force him over a mountain he hadn't wanted to climb.

Day by day he became more able to give thanks and believe his misfortune *would become* good in his own eyes.

This man's personality was changed. He reached such a peak of faith that his friends expected to see a new leg grow where the old one had been! But that wasn't his goal. He wanted God to be pleased with his faith. He saw his missing leg as being part of God's plan to spiritually fit him for eternity. With this faith came a greater appreciation for life and more inward peace than he had ever known.

Jesus knew this secret when He told us to leap for joy when we are hated and despised or when everything seems to be going wrong. (Matt. 5:11,12) He rejoiced to know that one day the Holy Spirit would help us to believe that God was working in and through all things.

Rejoice with Him whatever your situation is or becomes. As your expectations grow, you faith will move mountains! Soon you will be able to believe God for joys you have been letting slip away from you. Remember, God's rules are firm. We need only learn how they work — how to increase the level of our expectations.

Prayers with correct expectations are always answered.

Are you having a problem raising the level of your expectations?

An old Chinese proverb says, "A journey of a thousand miles begins with one step." That first step in learning how to increase our expectations could well be finding out why it is so hard to believe, when God *created us to believe*.

X

CREATED TO BELIEVE

Increasing our expectations is directly related to believing. Since God created us to believe, what is the bottleneck that stops the free flow of faith?

The question has haunted me as I have watched the desperate agony in the eyes of men and women who cried out for help.

"God, God, God, where are You? Why don't You help me?"

The memory of their haunting pleas for God to stop the pain that racked their bodies has kept me awake long hours on many nights. They weren't asking for wealth, power or luxury — only for help to fight against a horrible enemy that mocked them in their helplessness.

Nor were these the prayers of atheists or agnostics, but of

Christians who wanted to believe God — wanted to believe Him in sickness or in health — wanted to serve Him.

I have asked, "Why, God? Why? We are trying to believe You. We need to believe You. We are ordinary people who suffer here on earth, yet we don't know how to rise above our despair.

"You tell us to believe You and that by our faith, You will answer our prayer. But sometimes many of us can't seem to believe You. Why did you create us to be unbelieving, doubting, frightened souls?

"If I were creating man, I would have made it easier for him to believe. Faith would have been as natural as breathing — even easy. But You have made faith nearly impossible to attain."

I can feel their agony as I read the thousands of letters pouring in from all over the world.

"Help me, Merlin Carothers. God doesn't seem to hear my prayers."

And again, I would find myself before the Lord seeking counsel . . . some answer to the perplexity of this very real problem.

"Yes, God, I do believe You hear our prayers. I know You help me to believe You, Lord. But many people seem to be unable to believe. Their agony has become my agony and I need to know why they can't believe You."

It had all seemed so simple in the beginning, sharing the praise message. Then, as invitations poured in, my speaking ministry was soon taking up every spare hour I had. I was being invited to speak at hundreds of other places all over the nation.

The message of praise needed to be shared with as many thousands of people as possible, and I enthusiastically used every opportunity God provided.

Then came the gentle, yet firm prodding of the Holy Spirit, "Merlin, I want you to write. Write what I have taught you."

I was aware of no natural ability to write. Writing any

kind of book was beyond my wildest dreams, certainly beyond my ability. As for time . . . where would I find it?

After struggling with these thoughts, I finally said, "Okay, Lord, I'll write."

In me He had chosen a weak and unwilling vessel.

I could never claim to have been an all-wise author, and, if any book I wrote possessed any merit, it would be entirely thanks to God. But write I did and many thousands read what I wrote and wrote letters to me in turn, asking further questions about praise.

I had poured out of my heart every secret, every discovery, every answer God had ever given me. Eventually seven praise books had been printed in thirty-one languages around the world.

Many had been healed, lifted unto joy and set free from countless bondages. But what about the thousands of others who heard, and seemed to understand, but within hours or days were engulfed in doubt once more?

The healing, joy and peace they had claimed was gone. The fullness of the Spirit was within their grasp, yet they went away empty-handed. A life of confidence in God and themselves was closer than the very air they breathed, yet now gone — vanished — unreal.

They appeared to be free, and able to stand up and believe God for their needs and those of their families — able to ask God for anything. Able to receive all the endless promises He had given. Yet, back into the prison of discouragement they went.

The power wasn't working in them. Over and over I asked God to reveal to me the unfathomable mystery of why men and women could not seem to believe in Him.

True, answers to prayer and praise steadily increased. But it seemed that unanswered prayers also abounded. Many still floundered in despair. Now their agony threatened to destroy my own peace.

"Well, Lord, there must be something else. Maybe these people could be helped if I could only hear You more clearly. They want to believe You, but can't. Help me to understand why."

Answers did not come immediately.

I had to learn the lesson of faith that I knew others so desperately needed to learn. I had to believe that God was perfectly fair and just in all His dealings with man, and that He did hear my petition. His answer now seemed to be, "Wait on Me."

When His peace finally came to me, I knew He had all the answers and in His own time He would share them. I was at my desk one day, going through some routine work, when He spoke in the quietness of my spirit.

"Merlin, would you like to know why people find it so hard to believe Me?"

"Yes, Lord!" I responded fervently. "I really do want to know why You created people in such a way that they find it so hard to believe in You."

"I didn't,"came the firm answer.

I was momentarily at a loss for words, as the reality of this sank in.

"But, Lord, I've lived with people. I've seen their frantic struggles to try to believe in You. I've experienced these struggles myself."

"Think back a moment, to how man was when I first created him."

Then came a vision before me ... The Garden of Eden. Adam and Eve walking with God, believing Him. They did not know the meaning of doubt. What was there to doubt? God had set up all nature to cooperate with Adam and Eve, to bless them. Doubt was *unknown*.

But, when they disobeyed, the first seeds of doubt were sown in their hearts.

Each act of disobedience planted more seeds which eventually produced a harvest of doubt. Soon man became anything but a creature of faith. Doubt, watered with fear, made the human heart a garden of unbelief. God's enemy had taken the good soil created to produce good fruit and sowed the seed of discord. As this ugly crop matured, man sank into ever-increasing disobedience.

And now, here we are — by-products of this harvest of

disobedience. One part of us carries the mark of our created status — to believe. The other part — restless, resentful, questions God's right to tell us we must believe in Him.

"Give me evidence," the rebellious soul demands.

"Only believe Me," the Spirit encourages.

***

With this understanding came a glimmer of light in the midst of my confusion. We are not created to be agents of doubt! This was not God's legacy to man. He had no part in this failure.

Therefore, within man there is this ability, this natural quality of faith, however dormant and untapped.

I was reminded that God's Word says, " . . . according as God hath dealt to every man the measure of faith." (Romans 12:3)

So I realized that although this measure of faith has been submerged and covered up, it is still very much there.

But now I faced what seemed an even more insurmountable problem. How could I help others return to believing?

This weighed heavily upon my heart. Though it seemed I was on the very brink of a discovery that would help multitudes of people, it persistently eluded me.

Again I had to wait until my own heart was prepared to receive. Disobedience to God had been a very real part of my life.

I had heard and believed the commandment, "Thou shalt not lie" all my life. But when it had been more convenient to lie, I lied. I knew God had said, "Don't steal," but, if I had felt like stealing, I stole. I knew God commanded us not to use His name in vain, but if I was mad, the words came spilling out with little compunction. Then, as a Christian, I came to know that God wanted me to be patient and to let Him reveal His plan in His own time. But I walked in impatience more often than not.

Being willing to wait upon the Lord for His answers was

a part of the secret of faith I needed to learn. Only as I learned this could I share with others.

***

The life of disobedience so dulls the spirit that it is faith which seems unnatural. Doubt becomes the natural order of things. The disobedient mind has one thousand and one arguments against the principles of faith.

But the Spirit of God hovers near our spirit, ever watching for signs of our willingness to draw near to our Creator. And He encourages the faintest stirrings. He is ever true to His Word in James 4:8, "Draw near to God and He will draw near to you." For each step we take toward God, He takes two towards us.

That rebirth of believing has to be possible for *every* man. God's command is very simple. He leaves no loopholes — no excuses.

"Believe on the Lord Jesus Christ."

He knew we could and He left no room for our doubts. His requirement is absolute. Jesus said, "No man cometh to the Father unless he comes through faith in Me." (John 14:6)

Jesus was very firm about what was required for us to be able to receive *anything* from God. He said we must *believe*. No hedging. No equivocation — plain and simple, "according to your faith, be it unto you." (Matt. 9:29)

As the computer gives back to us what we have programmed into it, so does our faith. We get what we believe.

"Son, would you like to know what you can teach people that will help them to believe?"

Again He had spoken in a moment when I was not seeking an answer. It was as if He wanted me to understand that the answers were His gifts and not the result of any diligent soul searching or reasoning on my part.

"Yes, Lord," I waited expectantly.

"Teach men that in the same way they choose to disobey

Me, they must now choose to believe Me!"

There it was — so simple, yet it had completely eluded me.

What more logical solution could there be? I remembered the thought processes I had often used in disobeying God. If I knew something was wrong, yet strongly appealing to me, I had simply decided to do it anyhow.

Even though God's Spirit drew me toward obedience, my flesh pulled me toward disobedience. I willfully decided to disobey. I was programming myself for doubt.

Why not reverse the process? Decide to believe, even if my flesh said, "You can't believe."

Proof satisfies our flesh — faith satisfies our spirit.

The wise soul learns to say, "I do not seek understanding in order to believe. I choose to believe that I may understand."

Believing can become the natural part of man that it was created to be, for we have the ability to make the choice. A just God would never have required us to believe if He hadn't given us this capacity. Believing is as natural as breathing. WE ARE ALWAYS BELIEVING, EVEN IF IT IS NEGATIVELY!

Our bodies are equipped with lungs for breathing. Breathing is a life-and-death matter and God has provided special muscles to move the lungs, and ribs to protect them. If this special protection were destroyed, the body would die, for the breath of life would cease.

Adam was created possessing the power to believe God for anything. With this power Adam had perfect health and was in control of a perfect environment. How was he able to do this?

He controlled the world he lived in *by his faith* .

For example, animals were completely subject to him. And no weeds grew in Adam's garden. Anyone who has tried to eradicate weeds knows how destructive they are and how exhausting it is to try to control them. But Adam controlled them without any problem!

But the power in Adam to dominate and control was

contingent upon a special obligation he had to God. That obligation was obedience. Without obedience, the power vested in man would be short-circuited like an invisible force-field suddenly jammed and then withdrawn. Without this protective shield, Satan could freely rob and destroy man's God-given resources.

Man made a poor choice. A bad choice. He disobeyed God. From that moment, spiritual death settled like a shroud over man's spirit. The breath of spiritual life ceased when the special protective shield of obedience was destroyed. Man no longer controlled his body nor his environment.

Jesus obeyed perfectly so He could, even while in the flesh, control life, health, weather — even laws of gravity. He emphasized that we could do everything He did if we would be obedient to God.

Obedience, however, came not by following the laws of "thou shalt" and "thou shalt not", but by the new law of the spirit — the law of believing!

We have chosen to disobey God many times throughout our lives. The pull of the fallen nature has made it all too easy. We have disobeyed God in exactly the same way Adam and Eve did.

Now, we have the opportunity to reverse this entire process. Instead of disobedience, we can choose to obey — choose to believe. It won't be easy at first, but we *can* do it.

The exciting, thrilling part is that now we know we aren't facing an insurmountable task. We are simply returning to our original, created status, grounded in faith.

When our lives are in tune with God, we will be drawing on the greatest power source in all the universe. This means *positive* power for living!

The Holy Spirit can bring life and power back into man's deadened spirit and release the faith, long imprisoned behind a cold wall of disobedience. Throughout the Old Testament, the Spirit moved on men and helped them to believe. What had been dead in them came alive, just as the Spirit was released by Christ to raise the dead body of Lazarus.

Jesus revealed that soon the Spirit would move in the hearts of man in a new way, and God would then be *directly available to them.* Jesus said, "You can believe in Me and you shall do even greater works than I do." (John 14:12, paraphrased) In demonstration of this, Jesus breathed on his disciples and they received the Holy Spirit. Then they, too, performed many mighty works. And He is still breathing life into His followers.

Those first disciples received the power to be mighty witnesses for Christ. And they turned the world upside down! He wants to put that same power into our lives today, for we were created to believe!

XI

PROGRAMMED FOR SUCCESS

The reality of God's power, with which He wants to fill our lives, surrounds us. Take a look around you.

Have you ever wondered how God made this world? If you didn't know it was here, wouldn't you think it was impossible for anyone to create it? Absolutely impossible? But God created it out of nothing! He spoke it into being, using the very principles of faith which He told us will make ours an abundant life. And that which was not, became!

The vastness of the universe, in which there are as many stars as there are grains of sand on the sea shores, is beyond our comprehension. The existence of the universe would be difficult to believe if it weren't there staring us in the face.

How did God create it? What did He use to create something out of nothing?

Since God has placed such emphasis on our own faith, is it not reasonable to assume that faith is what life is all about? Jesus said that by our faith we could do anything.

God, by His faith, created all that we know. Our world, the whole universe, came into being and is held together by His faith.

In our lifetime, science has discovered that solid matter is not solid, as it appears to be. Instead it is composed of energy. A rock is actually energy united in a different molecular structure than air.

Now can see why God told us that we must believe Him. Everything He created is made of His own faith. By believing Him, we come into harmony with all that is.

What more logical thing could we do than to believe in the One who created us, even if we didn't know who He was? Wouldn't it be reasonable to put our trust in Him?

Jesus said, "Whoever has seen me has seen the Father." Jehovah has revealed Himself to us through His Son, Jesus. If we are able to believe that Jesus came from God, why not listen to what He told us? If we do this, we will be ready to believe Him in new and exciting ways. He said we have the power to believe. By believing, trusting and resting in Him, our entire lives are *re-created* to receive the abundant life He wants to give us.

Our reaction may well be, "That's for me!" Then we come up against old habits, ingrained in our lives, which hinder our progress.

Something has to go! We need to be reprogrammed! But how?

I want to share a very important fact that is as down to earth and relevant at this point as anything we will ever learn. It has to do with habits — both those we want to get rid of and those we want to develop. We get hooked on *anything* by doing it over and over.

A prime example is overeating. How frequently have we said, "Oh, I wish I hadn't eaten so much."

Logically, we should have learned our lessons. But when the next opportunity comes our way, we again eat too much. We strengthened the pattern — a pattern of eating too much whether we intended to or not.

Eventually such a pattern becomes so ingrained that we do it over and over without realizing what has happened. Usually we think, "It doesn't matter. I can stop any time I want to."

But as the years roll by and the pounds mount up, eventually the doctor says, "You are killing yourself with this excess weight." Then there is a frantic effort to lose weight. That, too, is soon forgotten, and it's back to the old pattern, the one we're "hooked on".

The person who drinks alcohol long enough will get hooked on it. (Some sooner than others.) He may deny addiction and, to prove it to himself, stop drinking. He suffers a period of self-denial, but when he thinks he has suffered long enough, he goes back to drinking.

I've watched such people "stop" drinking over and over. Eventually the stopping time gets shorter and shorter and the indulging time get longer and longer!

It's pretty apparent that whatever we do repeatedly becomes a habit.

Worry? Laziness? Oversleeping? Procrastination? These are all negative things.

Let's focus on some *positive* addictions! One positive addition in particular will help free us from negative addictions! It is closely tied in with all we have learned about praise.

Worshipping God!

Since we were created for this, it should be a supreme source of joy. I didn't say going to church or praying. I said, "*Worshipping God.*"

We can do this anytime, any place. But for it to become habit-forming, many obstructions have to be removed. When we hear the word "worship," our entire being usually reacts like this:

"Worship is something I should do. Something I do when I have to. But it's not fun and I'm not likely to get hooked on it!"

Little boys don't enjoy cigarettes either when they first

try them. Through burning, runny eyes and sputtering cough they wonder what's so great about smoking!? But it's the "in thing," so they keep trying. (No comparison to worship intended!) But it does illustrate the fact that we can learn to enjoy many things we at first dislike.

The supreme, ultimate pleasure of the human body, soul and spirit is found in worshipping God. Few people know this and most people would question its reality. But a man who hasn't climbed to the top of the mountain should never say he wouldn't enjoy being up there.

The joyful pleasure of worshipping god is known to far too few Christians. If we want to enter in, we are not likely to be crowded out by the mad rush of humanity!

To worship is to perform an act of reverence. Reverence is awe mingled with respect.

Have you ever seen a sunrise or a sunset that made you, for an instant, hold your breath? You were overwhelmed by its beauty. You may have thought, "Oh, if only an artist could paint that!"

Or have you stood atop a mountain and felt so exhilarated that it seemed you were in another world? Many people experience this the first time they look out over the vast expanse of the majestic Grand Canyon!

I have enjoyed this feeling often, floating through the air held up only by a parachute. It is a glorious feeling, impossible to adequately describe. Silently, the quiet broken only by the gentle rustle of the wind, I descend earthward. Like a giant bird high up in the sky, I float aloft, momentarily beyond the reach of the turmoil and chaos of the problem-filled world below ... peace ... serenity ... allow me to bask in exhilarating joy.

Worship is like this. A wonderful place of just resting in God. Realizing that He is here, with us, everywhere. Realizing that we "live and move and have our being in Him." (Acts 17:28)

Worship is at times being too filled with awe to speak. Of being lifted up above the problems of our world.

And at times, it can be wanting to shout, "Look!"

Although perhaps only we can see what there is to be so excited about. But it is enough, for God is in that moment and we feel more at one with Him, wishing the whole world could share the wonder of this revelation . . . of seeing, but being too overcome to be able to explain.

To worship is to adore — to love deeply. To love so deeply that we want only to be in His Presence. To worship is to learn how to be in His Presence and to enjoy being with Him so much that we never want to leave Him.

To worship is to revere and to adore Him so much that we know He will never leave us nor forsake us. To know that the power He used to create the universe is being incorporated now into everything we are involved in, "making all things work together for our good."

We worship Him, not because He could change water into wine if we should ask Him, but because water is always there when we need it. Not just because He is all-powerful, but because He never fails to supply what is best for us.

To adore Him is to trust Him completely . . . with the present as well as the future. *Today* He is with me, whatever is going on. Today is Sunday . . . worship day. But tomorrow, when I'm working in the rain, tired, hungry, misunderstood, disliked, loved, hated, despised, honored . . . that is today too. Today He is with me just as He promised. I'm worshipping in my spirit. I'm free. I'm in the world and yet not of the world.

How do we learn to worship, revere, adore?

To me, it's getting back to the basics. "Good morning, Lord. Thank you for the blessed new day."

Instead of, "Oh, I wish I didn't have to get up," try, "Thank you, Lord, that it's time to get up and go to work."

"Thank you , Lord, for this cold I've caught, for I know You are using the misery I feel to help me learn what I need to learn," instead of, "Why did You let this happen to me, Lord?"

"Thank you, Lord, for these bills I have to pay, for I know they are teaching me what I need to learn," instead of, "Oh, Lord, when will I ever get out of debt?"

Praising God did not come easily to me at first. I didn't see it as a pleasure or delight. It was a duty, pure and simple.

I wanted to get it over with and get on to "more exciting things." I was a doer — not a spectator. I didn't think of myself as being quite suited to the solitude of the life of worship. That was for the timid, the tired, the old.

Now I know that the timid, the tired and the old in spirit are too hooked on lesser things to want to come and get hooked on praising God. They have been filled to capacity with what they think they want out of life, by repeating it over and over. No one is going to rock their boat! Never mind that still waters may sometimes indicate stagnation rather than peace.

But let us be open enough to hear what the very Spirit of God is saying.

Jesus spoke of the Holy Spirit as joy. The Bible speaks of "fullness of joy". Jesus talked about finding something so desirable that a person would gladly sell all he had in order to possess it.

Have you discovered any pleasure worth giving up all you possess? Jesus did because He knew its worth, He tried in every way possible to pass it on to you and me.

Anyone who discovers what Jesus meant will be "hooked" forever.

Worshipping God is the eternal destiny of humanity and this eternal destiny is to be so glorious that we cannot even imagine what it will be like. Worshipping God will be the fulfillment of man's unending desire to find perfect, soul satisfying pleasure. This pleasure will not be dulled by enjoying it! It will only be increased! The sense of well-being that it provides will continue to increase for all eternity.

If praise and worship have this potential, we would be foolish not to begin practicing it now.

It may require us to struggle with past prejudices. But remember, Jesus promised that "he who has much will be given more." As we begin, He will add to that which we have, little though it now be.

We may be addicted to enjoying life only when everything is going well for us. This may have been our lifestyle for so long that breaking the habit seems impossible. The disciples frequently presented Jesus with logical reasons to be unhappy, but He never accepted them.

We were not created for unhappiness! Every unhappy thought or experience just "kills" us. Our stomachs hurt. Our heads ache. God wants something better for us . . . He wants us to always be happy.

But life isn't that way. Life is, I repeat, rough! Happiness is not easy to find in many circumstances. And perhaps in some, seemingly impossible. But remember . . . "With God, all things are possible."

Why not try God's perfect solution?

Practice worshipping Him *all* the time. Worship when you don't feel like it. When it seems dull, stupid, unreal. The body, mind and spirit will soon get the message. We have discovered what we were created for! And now we are on our way toward getting hooked on the most exciting experience in all the universe!

Worship by believing He is with us and controlling our situation. Must we wait until we feel His presence? If we wait for feelings, we will never really worship Him.

Feelings are controlled by our flesh. Worship is spiritual . . . of our spirit. "God is Spirit, and they that worship Him must worship Him in spirit." (John 4:24)

Jesus told the woman at the well, "The hour cometh, and now is, when the true worshippers shall worship the Father in spirit and in truth: for the *Father* seeketh such to worship Him" (John 4:23).

God is actually *looking* for people to worship Him in their spirits. For people who, deep within their beings, learn to adore Him.

Learning comes by doing! Praising is adoring. Praising is perfected through practice.

If we don't *feel* like praising Him, we can praise Him as a matter of choice, made by our *will* in obedience to our spirit. The flesh will eventually give in to the spirit, and will, in turn, become obedient to the leading of His Spirit.

Paul wrote, "We worship God in the spirit, and rejoice in Christ Jesus, and have no confidence in the flesh." (Phil.3:3) As we learn to disregard what our flesh dictates, and are obedient to His Spirit, we enter into worship. Paul entered into the delights of worship so completely that no matter what was going on in his life, he was "filled with joy". And think of the power he had in his life.

Jesus said, "I am come that ye might have life and that ye might have it more abundantly."

Think of the declaration, "*more abundantly*," being thundered out into space and reverberating throughout the universe ... increasing in volume and intensity as it reaches into eternity. Picture it passing the nearest star, thousands of light years away, and filling the solar system with the intense declaration of the Son of God. "*More abundant* ... LIFE MORE ABUNDANT!"

Temporal, earthly pleasures fade away with the end of this life, no matter how permanent they now seem. Abundance coming through Christ only increases with the end of this life. But we can get in on this abundance now. It's ours for the seeking.

He challenged us to seek, even though it wouldn't always be easy. He explained that our humanity is like the grass that withers away and if we live only in what seems to be pleasurable, we will be greatly disappointed.

Jesus emphasized that worship consisted not of the building of great buildings, or saying long prayers, or even doing many good things for others. He exhorted us to come and learn of Him.

Jesus gently, but firmly rebuked Martha for working so hard that she had no time to sit at His feet and listen. Mary chose to worship Him. Jesus said she had chosen the better part.

Martha, for all her "doing," became filled with frustration and complaints, which kept her from receiving the peace that comes from being in His Presence.

As Mary sat at Jesus' feet, listening and adoring, she could for the moment forget the cares and burdens of her day-to-day responsibilities and more clearly receive His guidance and direction.

Don't you suppose that if Jesus had said, "Mary, I would like a cup of cool water," she would have jumped to her feet and gotten it for Him? But she was doing what He wanted — listening, adoring, revering — trusting Him to let her know what He wanted.

Worship might involve "doing," but for most of us it involves first learning what He wants done. And what He wants most is that we first learn to love Him. And learning involves sitting at His feet and giving Him time to teach us. Trusting that He is in complete charge regardless of what "the Marthas" around us may think.

Worship is accepting the situation I am now in as my opportunity to learn, not continually begging God to make things different.

What would you give to hear Jesus speak just one audible word to you in His own voice? Think for a moment what it would mean to you to actually hear Him speak.

You can and you will.

His voice is the voice of His Spirit. His Spirit creates the reality of His Presence within. His Spirit causes His Words to take on life and meaning. Just as our breath is our life, the Word is God-breathed. His Spirit makes the Word come alive and we then experience what Jesus meant when He said, "My Words, they are spirit and they are life."

The Bible is very clear on this point:

"No one can really know what anyone else is thinking, or what he is really like, except that person himself. And no one can know God's thoughts except God's own Spirit. And God has actually given us His Spirit to tell us about the wonderful free gifts of grace and blessing that God has given us ... only those who have the Holy Spirit within them can understand what the Holy Spirit means ... but the spiritual man has insight into everything ... strange as it seems, we Christians actually do have within us a portion of the very thoughts and mind of Christ." (I Cor.

When God first created man's spirit, the spirit had no difficulty in worshipping God. The spirit ruled over and gave direction to the body and mind. Because of this divine order, there was perfect order and harmony on earth. There was no sickness, or pain, and man had abundance of all things.

God had told man that if he were disobedient, he would die. Man disobeyed and his spirit died. His mind thereupon began to tell the body what to do and the whole person began to suffer in body and soul.

The mind ungoverned by the spirit has no desire to worship God. The body doesn't want to either. To mind and body, worship is dull and lifeless. But this is because of the spiritual death which God warned man would experience as a result of disobeying Him. And this is still man's condition, until that time when the spirit is raised to life by God's Spirit and regains its rightful place of authority.

The disciples could not stay awake to pray with Jesus in the garden. He understood the problem — "the spirit is willing but the flesh is weak." The flesh, weak in understanding, wanted only to sleep. The spirit wanted to pray. But the disciples had not learned to overcome the lifelong habit of doing what the flesh wanted. And so they slept.

If you have received Jesus as your Savior, you have been born again. That new spirit within you wants to worship God. It is weak, but it can be strengthened, even in the most drastic cases.

I spoke with a man recently who had been a sailor for thirty years before he received Christ. His was a drastic case. Satan had been in control of his life all of those previous years and he had done exactly what his flesh dictated.

When this man came to see me, he did not look at all like a new Christian should. His eyes were bloodshot, his face red and deeply lined, his appearance one of evil. I could tell that he really wanted to follow Jesus. But he despaired of ever being able to.

As we talked about his life, a horrible and tragic story unfolded. He had been utterly in bondage to all Satan wanted him to do. Now it was evident, the Enemy would not give him up without a fight.

When he closed his eyes to sleep or pray, Satan would be there in front of him, leering and taking on the appearance of a ghastly and terrifying monster.

An evil presence would try to push him into sexual activity with the monster. Regardless of how he resisted, the evil suggestions would come to him — hour by hour, night after night.

To combat Satan, this man would resort to the old weapons of the flesh. He would curse him, damn him, swear at him and demand that he go back to hell! But Satan mocked him, and he grew increasingly miserable.

The man went to several different ministers who commanded evil spirits to come out of him, but he only grew worse. He went to psychiatrists, but they could not help him. In desperation, he caught a flight from San Francisco and came down to talk with me in Escondido.

It struck me, when we met, that this man still had a grossly wicked body and mind, and that his spirit was too weak to stand up and take charge of them. As I talked with him, I found many areas of his life that were not under control of the Holy Spirit. The Spirit showed me a picture that I could use to help the man. It was of a large ship that was infected with the dreaded black plague. I asked the man what needed to be done to the ship before it could be used again. He said it would have to be completely disinfected.

As I pressed him with this analogy, he realized that not just the deck of the captain's quarters needed cleaning, but every inch of the ship . . . from stem to stern.

Then I pointed out the areas of his life that were still infected by sin. Uncleansed of these, he was still subject to Satan's cruel whims. I explained that he had to begin immediately to build new thought patterns, desires and activities to change the evil patterns of his old life. I urged him to learn the words of Jesus so that he could quote them to Satan, rather than resorting to oaths and obscenities.

The man's face began to light up. I could see that he was already beginning to walk towards new freedom in Christ!

He realized that God had used me to help him find the solution. Others had hoped to solve all his problems for him in a single stroke. But that was not what he needed. Instead he needed to learn to make a habit of worshipping God in response to His mercy and goodness.

His old habits needed to be destroyed, and would be, as he received more of the mind of Christ. When his spirit realized this, the man began to change immediately.

He said, "I have hope for the first time in many years! When I accepted Christ I thought that was the end of all my troubles. When they didn't end, I was ready to give up. Now I see that I must and can become a new man. With His help I will!"

Few people have to deal with the deeply entrenched wickedness that characterized this man's life. But all of us have bad habits which make it difficult for our spirits to be free to worship God. Now the Holy Spirit wants to develop new habits, working through our own spirits, so that we are constantly being brought back to the order of our original creation. It will take eternity to completely deliver us, but our participation in eternity has already begun if we are born again.

Didn't Jesus say, "The kingdom of Heaven is within you"? And *it will be*, to the degree we let His Spirit bring us into continued worship and praise.

"Today is the first day of the rest of your life!" Grow in praise from this time forth.

Let your habit be to "rejoice in the Lord always". Seek new ways to worship so that your mind and flesh will be directed toward Him whether they want to or not. Let the Spirit be in control. He will enable you to respond to every situation with, "Praise the Lord!" This can be spoken aloud, or if circumstances prevent it , then it can be said in our hearts.

When I answer the telephone, I say, "Praise the Lord." This is good practice for me. It surprises some people and blesses others. And I must confess, it can be a little awkward when people call regarding business matters . . . even a little embarrassing at times. But I need to be embarrassed.

How do I know I need to be embarrassed? Because God promised to supply all I need; and if embarrassment comes to me, I must need it. When I hit my finger with a hammer, it hurts. I say, "Praise the Lord." My finger isn't pleased, but my spirit rejoices. God uses this experience to help me . . . just as He promised. (But I'd be very unwise to hit my finger on purpose just to see what good God might work out of it!)

Recently a young woman told me that she had left home because her mother was always so upset with her drinking, late hours, pot-smoking and loose living. When she occasionally went home for a visit, she couldn't stay long because of the worry and pain she saw in her mother's eyes.

Then the daughter had a devastating experience — pregnancy, abortion, rejection. She had nowhere to go and no one to turn to. She decided to make one more try at home and if she couldn't make it, she would end her life.

When she arrived at home, she couldn't believe what she saw. Her mother greeted her with open arms, laughing and with no trace of reproach in her eyes. Daughter's first question was, "Mother, what's happened to you?"

"I've learned to praise the Lord!"

"You've what?"

"I've been reading books on praise and I've been believing God is taking care of you."

The daughter wept as she told me how "at home" and loved she felt. When she told her mother about the pregnancy and abortion, she saw absolutely no reproach or worry in her mother's eyes. Only joy that she was home.

Then she told me, "I had to read what mother was reading . . . and my whole life changed!"

As she shared this, I could feel my spirit leaping within me. I was hearing about the power of the Holy Spirit. He is able to create life. He is the giver of life!

Let our prayer be: "Dear Father, let people see no condemnation in my eyes. Speak your love and hope where the need is greatest. Heal and make whole where hurt is deep."

As our bodies and minds learn to worship, our spirits will rise to their rightful place of authority. Only then can worship grow to be controlled by the Holy Spirit.

Sometimes people write and tell me my methods of teaching people to "praise the Lord" are too shallow, and that insincere or self-seeking praise is not worthy of being called praise. I agree that shallow praise is not worthy of God's blessing. It never will be. But then, did God save us because we were worthy?

God sees our unworthiness. Still He tells us to praise Him for everything. (Eph. 5:20) (Ps.150:6) He knew that we had become fleshly, carnal creatures.

God was willing to send His Son to suffer for us in order to redeem our spirits. He knew the power of the human spirit. Satan does, too. And that is why Satan reaches out to human spirits and uses them whenever he knows they are dominated by the flesh. He strengthens human flesh with the evil counterfeit knowledge, and in that condition man can do supernatural things which others are deceived into thinking are "from God". Under this evil influence, man can perform all sorts of signs and wonders. He can predict the future, bend nails with pure thought power, read minds, reveal past events and even heal the sick.

These counterfeit manifestations will increase as we near the coming of Christ.

Satan, true to his nature, comes to steal, kill and destroy. Jonestown saw the kind of devastation and destruction which are the end products of Satan's counterfeits.

God's gifts bring health and life. And "where the Spirit of the Lord is, there is liberty," not fear and bondage.

Once I unknowingly presented a counterfeit bill to a bank. It was mixed with several bona-fide bills. When the clerk said, "This one is counterfeit," my reaction was, "You're kidding!"

"No, I'm not. You will have to wait until I call the bank manager."

When the manager arrived, he said, "Where did you get this?"

"I don't have the slightest idea," I replied. "Somewhere between New York and California, in any one of a dozen different restaurants, hotels or banks."

"Well, you should have noticed it was counterfeit."

But never in my life had I even thought of looking for one. My lifelong habit had been to accept every bill at face value. Waiting at the bank until two representatives of the Secret Service arrived changed that habit forever!

They asked me dozens of questions, trying to help me recall where I might have picked up the worthless bill. I left without the bill, a little bit poorer and a whole lot wiser. Now I always look over anything larger than a twenty-dollar bill to make sure it's the "real thing", to make sure I'm not stuck with a counterfeit.

Jesus warned that by great signs and wonders, if possible, Satan will try to deceive even Christians (Matt. 24:24). Satan will use false prophets and anti-Christs to deceive many, but Jesus assures us that we will not be deceived if we are hearing His voice. As we grow in worship and praise, we will be able to discern His voice from that of error.

That which centers in Christ centers in praise to God. Through praise and worship, we enter into the right attitude for Bible Study, prayer, witnessing, giving, helping others and a dozen other useful activities.

Without praise and worship, we stagger blindly down many trails, never finding the abundant life God wants us to have. Praise to God prepares us for everything He wants us to do. It cannot be overemphasized, even though some choose to misunderstand.

I'm fully aware that some could use praise as an excuse for their own sin because they have misunderstood all that I have taught on this subject.

There will no doubt be individuals who sin and then casually "praise the Lord" for their sin. But they are only fooling themselves, for God reads our motives and intentions like an open book.

Many have also twisted the truth of salvation by faith and have used this as an excuse for their continued undisciplined and sinful lifestyle. But we are warned about using our liberty as an occasion to sin. (Romans 6:1)

Still, this misuse by some does not nullify the truth of salvation by faith. This doctrine was determined by God and whether we think He made a mistake or not does not change the absolute necessity of receiving eternal life by believing on Christ, rather than by thinking we can earn it by pious deeds and good works.

Praise and worship were decreed by God as the continual experience and "reasonable service" of all His children. He knew what we needed for real joy in living — now and in eternity.

Ephesians 1:11,12 reveals that our lives are to be gifts of praise to God. "... because of what Christ has done we have become gifts to God that He delights in, for as part of God's sovereign plan we were chosen from the beginning to be His ... God's purpose in this was that *we should praise God* ..." (TLB)

If it's that important to God, let's give it top priority in our lives!

XII

CHOOSE YE THIS DAY

The world is engaged in a violent struggle for survival. Jesus foretold the kind of times we live in ... "men's hearts failing them for fear of what is coming upon the earth". He told of perilous times, with wars and rumors of wars, until the very end of time. At the end, events would nearly extinguish mankind. The time we now live in has all the potential to fulfill the direst of these predictions.

Our world is like a powder keg waiting to go off. Those without the "peace that passes understanding", view the situation with increasing uneasiness.

Those who know the true source of peace, also know the true source of unrest. The real warfare we are engaged in is spiritual. Because this is so, forces will be unleashed eventually that have heretofore been unknown by mankind. The very foundations of the earth will be shaken.

Earthquakes, more powerful than any force ever unleashed by man, will rock the very foundations of our world. God is going to do what unbelieving humanity has been crying out for Him to do.

Man has asked, "If there is a God, why doesn't He do something about the terrible evil that exists in the world?"

God has put off this final destruction of evil for a good reason. In II Peter 3:7, 9, 14 (TLB), it is very plain: "Don't forget this, dear friend, that a day or a thousand years from now is like tomorrow to the Lord. He isn't really being slow about His promised return, even though it sometimes seems that way. But He is waiting, for the good reason that He is not willing that any should perish, and He is giving sinners time to repent. Remember why He is waiting. He is giving us time to get His message of salvation out to others." I'm glad He waited for me!

The last days will be more horrible than humanity has ever seen. According to Scripture, the blood of mankind will flow like a river.

But God will have the last word. "The day of the Lord is surely coming, as unexpectedly as a thief, and then the heavens will pass away with a terrible noise and the heavenly bodies will disappear in fire, and the earth and everything on it will be burned up." (II Peter 3:10)

On one momentous day, Moses warned the people of Israel to separate themselves from the tents of Korah, Dathau, and Abiram — men who had rebelled against Moses' authority. The people took this warning and cleared away from the dwellings. Then Moses spoke loud and clear and said that if the rebels died a normal death, it would be conclusive evidence that Moses did not bear God's authority. Thereupon the earth opened up and swallowed the rebels alive, but the people who had heeded the warning were spared. (Numbers 16:20-35)

Today the same sort of urgent warning comes to us because God is once again about to make a clear distinction between the righteous and the wicked as He visits mankind with the long-awaited judgement.

Whoever wants His protection and care should praise

Him for *everything*. Every breath we breathe and every thought that flows through our minds should be saturated with praise to Him.

God provided praise as the means by which we can place ourselves under His special protection, for the Scriptures indicate that God lives in the praises of His people. Those who live within the walls of His protection, His very Presence, cannot and will not have their spirits destroyed by evil forces that are unleashed in the world.

During the Boxer Rebellion in China, a lady missionary was captured and told to kneel down. They were going to cut off her head! The lady knelt as commanded; but as she did, she looked up into the face of her executioner and actually smiled. Witnesses reported that as she looked into his eyes, he seemed to be held spellbound. His face, that had been filled with anger and hate, changed. He took a few halting steps backwards, and then, along with his companions, turned and fled ... leaving the missionary alone.

The smile on that woman's face was an overflow of the peace she possessed within. There is power in God's peace.

If this woman had brought forth a concealed dagger and attempted to fight her way out of the problem, superior forces would have overwhelmed her.

Illustrations of the power of God are not limited to missionaries facing death in foreign lands. They are being played out in the every day lives of people just like you and me.

Forces around threaten to destroy us and may be far too powerful for us to physically defeat them. They may not try to cut off our heads, but they threaten to destroy our peace of mind and joy of living.

Those observing the missionary lady's plight may have thought it ridiculous of her to look upon her captors with a smile. Ridiculous or not, she smiled, and God used her peace to win a victory for her and His kingdom.

This is the same power He made available to Shadrach, Meshach and Abednego when they were thrown into the fiery furnace. They refused to be afraid. It was there that they met "the fourth man" in the furnace of their affliction — Jesus. Not a hair on their head was singed by the fire nor was the smell of smoke even on their clothes when they were delivered out of the fire.

When Jesus looked fearlessly upon those who had come to arrest Him, they fell back to the ground in fear.

Evil is able to attack those who are afraid, but it is helpless in the face of peace. If we attempt to attack our problems with an effort generated by fear or anxiety, we will know only defeat.

It is true that men and women who have been afraid have taken up arms and defeated those who attacked them. This works whenever the weapons we use are stronger than those weapons which come against us. But, sooner or later, all of us will be attacked by forces too strong for any weapons we may possess. Then we must trust in His power. We will face certain defeat if we trust in any other.

If we are in a situation that is too difficult for us to handle, we have great reason to rejoice! This is our opportunity to learn to put to use the very power that Jesus used, and said would be available to us.

Our flesh would like to have the resources to squash everyone and everything that would come against us, but our spirits long instead to see the power of the Creator working in us.

Most of the time, Jesus walked as any man would walk. While He occasionally walked on the water, He did not always demonstrate power we would consider miraculous.

I think of Jesus as *being* all power. He didn't use it as an "escape mechanism" when the going got rough. During His wilderness experience, He refused to make bread out of stones, although He was hungry. God does not promise to always miraculously deliver us from death or problems, but He wants us to abide in His power — to know and believe it is there.

The enemies we face may not be guns or swords. They may be a husband or wife or friend who has turned against us, and we feel unable to do anything about it. Everything we have tried may have been unsuccessful and we feel completely defeated.

Rather than retreat in defeat, now is our opportunity to advance in victory! Advance with the mighty weapon of praise on our lips, knowing that God is abundantly able to dissolve our problems — or to sustain us *in* them.

Our enemy may be an evil habit that has wrapped its ugly tentacles around our lives, threatening to squeeze every drop of joy out of us. Perhaps we have attempted to defeat this enemy with every resource we had available and found they weren't enough.

Rejoice that through Christ we *are* victorious. Jesus said that *in His name* we could do anything. Believe that, and our spirits are free. More of His power is flowing!

***

A woman faced the horrible enemy of mental illness. She had been committed several times to mental institutions, but had not been helped. Each time she was released, she was kept on medication that made her life nearly unbearable. Her family lived in continual fear of what she might do to herself. She was unable to be of any support or benefit to her husband or to her children.

Then a friend gave her a copy of *Prison to Praise*.

As she read the book, a little light began to penetrate the darkness of her depression.

She decided to step out in faith and thank God for everything in her life, precisely as it was: her situation, her problems and difficulties. Power began to be released into her very weak life.

Amazing things began to happen!

Mental confusion and fear faded away. Fear could not withstand the quiet confidence and peace that were growing in her.

Today, she is completely free of tranquilizers and medication of any kind, living a normal, healthy and productive life.

His Power had set another "captive" free.

***

Leslie believed in God and often prayed that He would protect her family wherever they might be. But she had stopped going to church, seeing little need to worship God in that way.

One evening, when Leslie was riding in her cousin's car, he stopped behind another car to assist a stranded motorist. As he stood there between the two vehicles, trying to decide how he could help, a third vehicle driven by an intoxicated young woman suddenly seemed to come out of nowhere! As it loomed out of the darkness at a dangerously high speed, it ran off the edge of the highway, ramming the back of her cousin's car. He was caught between the two cars, his legs so violently jammed between the bumpers, that the lower half of one leg was completely severed!

He somehow survived the frantic trip to the nearest hospital and the agonizing four-hour wait for surgery.

When Leslie got to the hospital the next day, her cousin's first words to her were, "Praise the Lord." His attitude was one of cheerful optimism and complete forgiveness of the young woman who had caused the accident.

Leslie was completely taken aback! She could not understand his peace of mind in the midst of this senseless tragedy! She was too shocked to even discuss his "ridiculous attitude" with him! But she had to admit to herself that her cousin was one unusual man.

Later he gave her copies of *Prison to Praise* and *Power in Praise*, encouraging her to accept Christ. And she did. His witness overcame her previous reservations.

A high price to pay for the salvation of one woman? No higher than the price God paid for each one of us to receive eternal life.

***

Terry was on the critical list in a hospital in Las Vegas, Nevada. He had been in a severe automobile accident. The doctors said he had the worst brain damage they'd ever seen. He could never recover. For as long as he lived, he would be a vegetable.

Terry went through numerous problems — blood clots, staph infections, kidney infection and pneumonia. Things looked bleak, to say the least.

However, members of Terry's family had learned there is a power far greater than disease and disaster. They began to thank God *for* Terry's affliction and for his condition ... just as it was.

The doctor had gone into Terry's room every morning for three months, and was accustomed to speaking to him as if he could hear. "Good morning, Terry." But Terry had never responded. And the doctor hadn't really expected him to.

Then, one morning shortly after members of Terry's family united to draw upon "praise power", the doctor entered the hospital room with his usual, "Good morning, Terry".

"Good morning, Doctor!"

The doctor stopped in his tracks. This was unreal! But there was no denying the reality of what he was hearing. For next, Terry asked where he was, where his wife and family were and how he gotten in this room!

Terry went on to make a rapid recovery, in spite of every dire prediction that he "would never recover".

God doesn't know the meaning of "never". And it's not likely to enter our conversation either when we are praising the Lord.

Terry could have died, *or* recovered, but neither would have changed Jesus' positive command, "Let not your heart be troubled ... I have overcome ... "(John 14:1)

The natural response to calamity of one kind or another is fear, anxiety and inner turmoil. But to the best of my knowledge, neither fear nor turmoil has ever resulted in a miraculous cure of anything. But there are countless instances when God's power has been released as someone exercised his faith by praising Him.

***

I went to grammar school with a girl named Esther. Years later she was happily married to a man she loved with all her heart. He was all she had ever hoped for. He was a hard worker, kind, gentle, and a very dedicated family man.

They were happy together, though neither attended church or gave God any part of their lives. They didn't seem to need Him. More accurately, they had not encountered the sort of problems which necessarily would turn their thoughts to a power greater than themselves. And life seemed good.

In the midst of their idyllic life, her husband, Jim, got up one morning feeling ill. They knew something was *very* wrong with him.

During a long year of tests and examinations, doctors made a wide variety of diagnoses. First they diagnosed heart attack in the form of two slight strokes. Later they thought he had a brain tumor with a ninety percent chance of recovery.

During this whole time, Jim was hospitalized. Having a lot of time on his hands, he began to read the Bible for the first time in his life. He received Christ as Savior.

Though his body was so weak that he could barely move himself, he would manage to get on his knees and express thanks to God. He never complained. His wife was baffled by this "new Jim". She decided, "He has flipped his cork!"

For Esther, life was not so calm. She was bitter and in her resentment she kept asking, "Why did this have to happen to us!!?"

One day she went into a grocery store and, while browsing through a newly-installed revolving book rack, she saw the name, Merlin R. Carothers.

"Now that couldn't be the Merlin Carothers I went to

school with," she thought to herself. But she was interested enough to purchase a copy of *Prison to Praise*. She soon realized that it was indeed the same person. She read on with renewed interest.

She told me, "Before I finished that small book, I knew I was becoming a new and different person inside. I sat, long after I'd finished reading, and just loved Jesus, and could even thank God for allowing Jim's illness, but most of all, for showing me the right way. It's wonderful!"

She also wrote, "Merlin, my heart was broken and I thought that there was no medicine for it. But oh, there is!"

***

Pauline was in constant pain night and day. She had been on pain medication for several months. Finally, the doctors decided she would have to have a complete hysterectomy.

After the operation, she was in even greater pain, and was kept under heavy sedation with shots and pills. A friend named Iola came to visit her and brought a copy of *Prison to Praise*.

Pauline was in far too much pain to be interested in reading. She left the book by the bedside, unopened.

When she finally went home, Pauline was kept on a continual round of pain pills every four to six hours. She was so miserable that finally, one day, hoping to find momentary escape from her ever-growing frustrations, Pauline picked up the book Iola had given her and began to read.

When she reached page seventeen, she began thanking God for her condition because she realized He had a purpose for what had happened to her. She kept reading, until she just couldn't keep her eyes open another minute. She drifted off to sleep with words of praise skipping through her mind.

The next morning, she awakened feeling like a brand new person! She got up, went into her kitchen and did the dishes. That felt so good, she decided to dust the furniture.

All the time she realized she was feeling the best she had in years! The words of praise and thanksgiving that had filled her mind as she drifted off to sleep the night before, now came bubbling out as songs of praise!

She couldn't wait to call her family to tell them the wonderful thing that had happened to her! Her younger sister said, "Pauline, have you been taking too many of those pain pills?"

"Why no. In fact, I haven't taken any today," was Pauline's joyous reply. "God has healed me because of my praising Him!"

She then called her son and his wife and shared the good news with them too, urging them to bring their new baby over. It had been a long time since she had felt like being around a noisy, active grandchild, but now she could hardly wait to hold her granddaughter! As soon as they arrived, she was able to pick up her smiling granddaughter and dance around the room with her!

Her younger sister, Henrietta, came over and remarked that the pain she had seen in Pauline's eyes for months was completely gone.

Whenever Pauline would tell her family all she was doing, they would inevitably caution her, "Now Pauline, don't overdo it."

She just laughed and assured them, "But I feel better than I ever have in my whole life."

The more she praised the Lord, the better she kept feeling.

Pain is a direct result of man's fall. And God is able to release His mighty power to cancel pain. He may not *always* choose to do this, but the most beautiful and effective way to give Him the opportunity to release His healing power is to praise and thank Him.

There are times when, for our own benefit, God does *not* choose to relieve us of all pain. He chooses rather to let us suffer in the flesh in order that we might grow in our spirits.

For example, when a child touches a hot stove the pain

warns him of serious danger. The child begins to realize that when mother or father says, "No, no," it is for a good reason.

Some children seem to have to learn the hard way, though God would not have it so. We can avoid the hard way if we do as James 4:8 says, "Draw near to God and He will draw near to you."

Many times, we refuse to draw near to God until we are in serious trouble, so He has to allow us to go through an experience that will cause us to want to draw near to Him. (Even more tragic than going through some traumatic experience though, would be the tragedy of never seeing our need for Him.)

On the other hand, there are pains we suffer needlessly — pain that God never intended us to bear — the pains of anxiety, worry and fear. This kind of pain does *not* work for our benefit.

Satan loves to have us suffer needlessly and harmfully. This suffering never gives us or anyone else an advantage.

As praise brings us into God's presence, so fear and anxiety drive us out of His presence.

The power of praise defeats this sort of pain so we can endure physical pain, when we must, with a sense of peace, confidence and faith in God. Then He will make pain work for our benefit and not to our detriment.

This is real power — power we can ill afford to be without.

XIII

INCREASE YOUR EARNINGS

If I could show you how to increase your earnings twenty-five dollars a week without having to do any more work, you would be interested. It wouldn't make you a millionaire overnight, but most of us could use an extra twenty-five dollars if the income entailed no risk.

If the plan I showed you increased your earnings by fifty dollars each week, for the rest of your life, you would be even more interested. If I demonstrated ways to double or even triple that weekly increase, I would have your undivided attention.

And if I introduced you to a thousand people who had tried my "system" and proven it to be absolutely trustworthy, wouldn't that motivate you to spend at least a little time and effort to learn it? I'm sure it would.

Occasionally people try the principles of praise and expect to be instantly on top of the world with no more problems. It doesn't work that way. It's not some "get rich quick" scheme. Praise is a positive, Scriptural way to make everything in your life work *for* you instead of against you.

For instance, how do you react when someone walks right to the front of a line when you have been waiting your turn, and rudely crowds in ahead of everyone else?

You have several options. You can grab the offender and show him where the end of the line is! But in case this is not your style, you may be the type who just stands there and glares angrily at him.

More than likely, such a rude person will be oblivious to the angry "vibes" you're sending his way as he finishes his business and goes on his way. But for yourself, the rest of your time waiting in line will be miserable as you inwardly boil at the "rudeness of *some* people"!

Your heart beats a little faster. The excess acid your stomach begins pumping out begins to burn. Your head begins to throb with the first signs of a headache.

Or perhaps you experience no symptoms, but your internal system sets off a silent alarm that signals your body to be prepared for trouble if any more stress develops.

I would like to propose a better way to handle this kind of situation.

When someone steps in line ahead of you, turn on the praise principle. Thank the Lord for bringing that person into your life to be used to supply something you need. Go the second mile and ask God to bless him. As Jesus said, "Bless your enemies." As you begin to respond with the mind of Christ, the blatant rudeness that confronts you will not bother you quite as much.

The next time this sort of thing happens, you are better prepared. You remember how you were able to thank the Lord for that "line-bucker" and how it kept the lid on your anger and preserved your peace of mind. This time, you are even able to smile a little. Eventually the rewards increase.

For example, you begin to see beyond the rudeness. You can begin to reflect on how hurried and anxious rude people are, and on how little respect they must get from others. You meditate on how faithfully God provides all your needs, giving you the sort of security that makes it unnecessary for you to push in front of others. His peace grows in you as you let His Spirit more and more direct your spirit.

I haven't shown you how to be a hilariously happy person yet, have I? No. That is not my immediate objective. What I have shown you is how to make praise work for you a little more.

With the principle of praise you are able to take every event in your life and make it work for your good. This has to be worth quite a lot. And you have the benefit of knowing that as thousands of other people have tried praising God for everything, good resulted.

It costs you nothing to believe God will take everything and work it for your good — absolutely nothing. But its benefits will steadily increase.

Every time you are successful in believing that some frustrating event will actually work for your good, you are growing in the ability to make your faith work in more difficult circumstances. And the benefits keep increasing.

Eventually your trust in God becomes a powerful force. God wants you and me to be happy and so He has built into this world unlimited resources to bring happiness. The power in praise is one of His free gifts. Every new discovery, even in science, is simply man's finding what God has already provided for us.

Christians *should* be happy — but often aren't. Too often, many have either lost their happiness *or* never discovered what it is like to be truly filled with His joy.

Now why would I be concerned with your happiness? Let me tell you! Happy Christians draw non-Christians to Christ.

I once thought the "power of the Holy Spirit" enabled one to speak loudly enough to tell people with compelling force that they needed to accept Christ. Now, however, I know that power means having what it requires to convince someone to accept the Lord Jesus. To *convince* someone means more than telling him, "You should come to Christ." It means being the kind of person who will cause others to *want* the peace we have.

People have a natural, God-given desire for happiness. They will spend all their earnings and quite a bit more to try to find it. Actors and actresses are paid millions of dollars to look and act happy. But I've seen how they react when the cameras stop rolling and the lights are cut. Drained of huge amounts of energy to put across their "happiness", they collapse in their dressing rooms and reach for a drink!

Acting happy is a real strain if you aren't happy. Sometimes actors become so drained that they cannot face real life any more and some have even left us with the message, "Stop the world, I want to get off!" And they do. We read about it in the headlines.

Man is continually looking for ways to be happy, but what he really needs is peace. God wants us to find a peace so great that it is actually beyond our understanding.

It is glorious to lead a Christian into a better understanding of the gifts of the Holy Spirit, or to pray for one who is sick and to see God heal him. But I'm finding it even more wonderful to teach Christians how to be filled with His peace. Such a Christian becomes a light, going out and winning others to Christ.

Jesus said that we are to be like a lamp, giving light to all who are in our presence. Because this is so, our faces should radiate His joy, "as though a floodlight is beamed upon you." (Luke 11:36 — TLB)

People will see this light and be drawn to look closer . . . and to wonder . . . "Why are you so different from others?"

As we learn the secrets of praise, we are able to enter into His peace. You may have been a Christian for a long while but still be an unhappy person. You will not be a light in the world if you are unhappy. But praise will take all that has made you unhappy and make it work for you.

Praising God centers our attention on Him instead of on our problems, causes our faith to grow, fills us with His peace, and makes us radiate His joy.

106

Have you ever noticed that the gospel has little effect on people who are not looking for it? People, for example, who are looking for a good time, usually don't think they will find it in "religion". If we start "preaching" Jesus to them, they tune us out.

Countless Christian parents have tried to force their children to become Christians. But it never works. Children want fun and spend most of their time and energy looking for it. They will break the rules of home and society in order to find what looks like fulfillment to *them*!

Parents should be a light to their children. And they can be a light to children simply by learning to be at peace. Every child knows what Jesus has or has not done for his parents. The fact that you go to church, pay your tithe and obey the laws will not make your child want to follow you, if he sees that you are unhappy.

I can almost hear the response to this.

"But it isn't Jesus who makes me unhappy! It's my husband or wife, or my job, or my health."

That may be true, but Jesus promised to give you joy and peace that *passes understanding*, regardless of what was going on around you. Has He kept His promise to you?

If not, you need to learn how to receive it. You need to learn to praise. I do not promise you that it will be easy to learn. All I can promise you is a life that experiences and expresses "fullness of joy" — a life that will draw others to the Lord Jesus.

When your mate or children or friends anger you, disappoint you, ignore you, etc., etc., this is your opportunity to learn.

Don't strike back in kind. Return good for evil. And make your response as genuinely loving as you possibly can.

This releases God's power in you. Others can see what you are doing and are deeply impressed. They won't see such things happening in the world!

People long to see peace demonstrated. And the more you respond in peace, the more the Holy Spirit will actually change you. Others will want to know the source of your peace — Jesus.

Jesus was fast asleep in a small boat while a storm was frightening His disciples. He was so at peace that, although He could understand why they were frightened, He rebuked them for their lack of faith.

***

We could stand on a street corner for the rest of our lives, shout the good news of the gospel and have no one pay attention. In fact, Satan himself would even ignore us. He doesn't care what we do unless our activities begin to influence someone else! When our lives start making others think about Christ, then Satan pays us very careful attention.

Praise has unlimited power, and it can win every person in your family to Him. If that is important to you, learn to praise Him.

Remember — unbelievers are looking for examples of Christ's handiwork. We may never know they are watching us. But our lives can motivate them to seek Him, if we let His light shine through us. If we have been a 25 watt light bulb, we can let Him make us into a 100 watt bulb!

Because the darkness all around us is great, the need for light is great. So when trouble comes — shine.

When people see that Jesus makes our problems work for our good, our light grows brighter and brighter, until it increases in brightness from a 100 to a 300 watt bulb.

Because the source of power is unlimited, we can continually increase our wattage as we allow praise to release the power in us. This is why Paul said, "Rejoice always!"

Even when no unbelievers are around to see us, we need to keep undergoing change. Then, when the light is really needed, it will already be shining brightly. In fact, there's no use trying to pretend we are filled with praise just to impress an unbeliever. Praise in secret until it becomes real.

Praise will show in our eyes. This light can't be hid, and it can't be imitated. It is a solid conviction that God is working *all things* for our good, so we are rejoicing in all things.

Paul practiced this joy in prison when very few people could see or hear him. He then lived it when many others were around, and won countless people to Christ. I'm with Paul. How about you?

We can win people to Christ whom we may never see or know. People who want desperately to believe that God does help people ... people just like themselves.

We are surrounded by a "cloud of witnesses" closely watching us to see if we have anything really worthwhile. I will never forget the reality of what I saw in the life of a young man seriously wounded in Vietnam.

Both legs were gone. Blood-soaked bandages covered the stumps well above what had once been knees. One arm was completely gone. He was blind. Bandages covered the gaping holes where once his eyes had been. My only link with this man was through his hearing.

"Tell him to thank Me that he is exactly where he is," I seemed to hear the Lord say.

"God, I can't do that! Please don't ask me to tell this pitiful being to be thankful for this. He wouldn't understand — I myself don't even understand."

"Tell him."

God was preparing me. What an agonizing way to learn, but God knew what I needed. And He knew what this young man needed, who had become one of the worst living casualties of the Vietnam War. He was in hell. I was learning how to help men who are thrust into suffering.

"But does God cause terrible things like this to happen?" I am often asked. No! Satan is the source of such pain and suffering, but God has promised to use everything Satan does for blessing instead of cursing, if we would trust Him.

The soldier wanted to die. The doctors said his desire would probably cause his death. The human part of me wondered if that wouldn't be best!

As I told that boy about praising God, he confessed, "I don't even believe in God!"

Here was my clue. This man would receive eternal life if I would praise God for him. My feeble faith took hold and I believed God would use this tragedy for the man's good.

As I urged the soldier to praise God, he slowly responded, and, after several days, he joined me in prayer. He said, "Oh, God" ... just that ... "Oh, God," ... over and over.

As the man's faith grew, he accepted Christ as his Savior. One day he said, "The way you kept praising God helped me to believe in God myself."

He accepted his physical infirmity as a stairway to eternal life. And through him, God reaffirmed the power of praise. That soldier became the irrefutable witness for Christ among the worst skeptics. I watched doctors who had previously shown no interest in God, change their attitudes completely. They were seeing faith build life in the face of death and despair.

One doctor told me his own life had been empty, even with two good legs, two arms and perfect vision. He said, "I see in this wounded man a joy of living that I don't have."

A corpsman said, "I've been against 'religion' of any kind for years, but this man has gotten to me."

The more severe the problem, the heavier the burden, the greater potential it has to bring others to faith in Christ. As God permitted His own Son to be attacked by Satan, He still permits us to suffer if He knows the suffering will either help us or bring others into His Kingdom.

You were born in your country, into your family and your situation — that the needs God saw in your spirit might be met. So believe He is using even the slightest detail in your life for your sake. Nothing is insignificant.

Rejoice in that fact by faith and God will make it so.

As your praise points others to Him, He will not fail to honor your trust. Your life is proving to the "cloud of witnesses" that they, too, can trust Him.

XIV

CLOUD OF WITNESSES

God used the twelfth chapter of Hebrews to give me a new understanding of the kind of witness He wanted Merlin Carothers to be. I was amazed to see what the Holy Spirit revealed was wrong in me. It had never occurred to me that I was so flagrantly disobeying His Word.

Let me explain. When I hurt, I wanted others to share my burden of pain with me. It seemed only natural. If I had a headache, others should know about it so they would take it easy on me.

So what if I felt crabby or irritable; it was only fair for people to know about it. The least they could do was to be a little understanding! After all, it wasn't my fault I felt bad. I didn't ask for it.

And if I felt provoked, it was only logical to me that the

person responsible was to blame. If I didn't feel like being pleasant to the world, that was my business. So watch out, world! This is not one of my good days!

Looking back, I'm thankful that the Lord knew just the right time to reveal His will for me. Had it come earlier, I wouldn't have been ready.

This must be the right time for you, too — since He arranged to speak to you through the pages of this book.

As you read this chapter, it could influence how you think and what you say for the rest of your life.

You have heard the expression, "You can't see the forest for the trees." Our sins are pretty much like that. We tend to see them as individual and isolated items. And, if we steal or lie or commit adultery, we have no difficulty identifying these acts as sin. But seldom are we able to stand back and see the subtle intertwining of the web of sin that may constitute a sizable aspect of our personality. It's usually a pattern of behavior that's been with us for so long, it seems a natural and acceptable part of our lives. We forget that what seems natural for us, may be quite repulsive to God. Repulsive, because we are so far from the way He intended us to be.

The very first word of Hebrews 12, "Wherefore", refers to the previous chapter, where the writer told us about the men who had borne glorious witness to the world because of their faith in God. They had believed Him when all evidence seemed to say He was not doing what He promised to do. It all looked so impossible.

Noah built the ark when there wasn't the least sign of a coming flood. In fact, it had never rained in all of history until that time.

Abraham left his home and journeyed into a foreign land, without knowing what awaited him. He was willing to put everything on the altar of trust — even his beloved son, Isaac.

Moses was willing to lead approximately two million people out into the wilderness with no security other than God's promise to him. It had to be quite a step of faith for Moses with not even a supply train to take care of their needs.

The people had to move out in blind faith. This wasn't easy for them, but God had called each of them just as surely as He had called Moses at the "burning bush".

Every example in Hebrews 11 is of a man or woman who trusted God without visible evidence of how He would keep His promises. Their examples of faith assure us that God can be trusted, even when we can't see Him or He seems not to be speaking.

"Now faith is the substance of things hoped for, the evidence of things not seen." (Heb. 11:1)

Our lives can provide this kind of testimony to those around us! God glories in anyone who will trust Him. Your life and work are as important to God as those of anyone else in the whole world. He does not need "big people". But He does need people *big in faith* — people who trust Him.

When Paul speaks in Hebrews 12 of being compassed about by a great cloud of witnesses, he is employing the imagery of the ancient Greek athletic contests in stadiums filled with spectators. The contender was compassed about by so many people, they were like a cloud all around him. The eyes of all were fixed upon him as he strove to win. Everywhere he looked were banks of people, their attention firmly riveted on him.

We, too, are compassed about by people who are watching. They may be very near to us, at home or next door. Or they may be a little farther away, observing us at work, school or church. But they are all around us, watching.

Bear with me here, because this is important. I suspect you've heard more than one sermon about the importance of the quality of the testimony our life gives to the watching world. But what I have to share next is, I think, something you have not heard before.

All my life I thought the cloud of witnesses were people watching to see if I committed the easily-observable sins, such as drinking, smoking, swearing or immorality. However, I know now that was a mistake. Paul tells us to "lay aside every weight." (Heb. 12:1)

As Christians we are to prepare ourselves so that we can, will all possible speed, move toward the goal God has for us. So we need urgently to know *exactly* what Paul means when he tells us to "lay aside every weight and sin which clings so closely." (RSV)

In what sense does sin cling closely to us? This speaks of sin that has everything in its favor, including time, place and opportunity. It has to be so close that it is frequently committed and so favorably situated we can do it over and over. In fact, the opportunity comes to us from every direction.

Can you see that this sin does not fit the pattern of murder, stealing or immorality? This sin has to be so common that it is constantly hanging around the fringes of our lives.

A runner looks to the finish line, even as we are to be "looking to Jesus" as our goal. In the text we're looking at, the writer described Jesus as "the author and finisher of our faith". The same Greek words translated here as author and finisher were also used to specify the judge of an athletic competition. Jesus awards the prize for the contest we are in, because He Himself entered competition and won. He ran the race to show us how He wanted us to run our race.

"He, for the joy that was set before Him, endured ... " (Heb. 12:2)

He set His attention on the goal and joyfully endured whatever God required of Him. He "despised the shame". But being shamed meant nothing to Him in order that He might make it to the finish line and sit down with His Father. He did not consider obstacles in His path as worthy of His concern.

He endured.

When Hebrews 12:3 speaks of the "contradiction of sinners against Himself," it means He was spat on, beaten with a rod, lied about, denied, betrayed, forsaken. What was He tempted to do through all these things?

He was tempted to "be wearied and faint in (His) mind." (v.3) This was the temptation that surrounded Him, but which He never gave in to. All of these things were as

114

nothing to Him, in comparison with the prize.

Why?

It was important to God that Jesus be totally committed to trusting Him. Abraham, Moses and Noah had trusted God, but always after God convinced them.

Jesus needed no convincing.

He knew the race was part of God's plan for Him and He set His face toward the finish-line. If He encountered obstacles in this marathon race, He never asked, "Why me, God?"

Man was never to see Him falter. Satan was never to see Him flinch. Satan thought he had won, but God took the vile scheme meant to destroy Jesus and mysteriously turned it into the most blessed event in all of history.

Right from the beginning, Jesus knew what was coming. But He accepted it with faith in His Father. We are being challenged to do the same.

Paul points out that chastening of any kind — those obstacles which we encounter in our race — may seem to be grievous but for God's children they always result in good.

God has put His Son's name on the "bottom line". He will not permit His Son to be ashamed! If Satan could ever prove that God failed to use even one event for good in the life of those who trust Him, Christ's victory would be shattered! But never once has our adversary succeeded in proving a failure on God's part.

The temptation that surrounds us and clings so closely is the temptation *to be weary*. It seems so natural to be weary. The temptation is like a wall around us, hemming us in from the victory that should be ours in Christ. This besetting sin is so subtle that we give in to it over and over, almost without realizing what is happening.

We have a ready excuse, "But I'm only human. I can't be perfect." That's true. We aren't perfect, but we are perfected. And we should strive to be like Him. He has already demonstrated the "how to." We need only affirm, "I can do all things through Christ, who strengthens me." (Phil. 4:13)

The result?

"Those who wait upon the Lord shall renew their strength; they shall mount up with wings as eagles; they shall run, and not be weary; and they shall walk, and not faint." (Isa. 40-31)

He is looking for people who will not turn away from Him when the going gets rough. He is asking them to do what they do not want to do — think they cannot do. He is looking for those who will turn to Him, draw new strength from Him and keep running the race!

Jesus trusted His Father one hundred percent! He always spoke with powerful enthusiasm about God's plan for His life. And His enthusiasm was not focused on a distant goal — something by and by.

It was His claim for the "here and now".

Now I am in God's will.

Now God is working in me.

Now I have no place to lay my head and own nothing because this is what He wants of me.

Now I will be betrayed, denied, crucified because this is His will for me. But I want His will, because He is always right. And because I know this, He always answers my prayers!

Jesus didn't ask God to change the weather because He didn't happen to like the wind and storm. For Him, the wind and storm were God's will. He could peacefully sleep, even when the ship was sinking. And because He *was* at peace, He *could* change the weather. But He did it only to benefit the disciples.

With His help, I am learning the benefits of trusting Him. But it isn't always easy. This besetting sin that surrounds me doesn't want to accept the *now*. It wants to reject *now* and cries out for something different. It tempts all of us to reject God's will for *now* to *let others know* that we reject it.

Letting others know is an important part of "the sin". We show them, this cloud of witnesses, that we are not accepting God's will with joy. We show them that we do not

116

despise (ignore as nothing) the problems we have. Instead we are plainly upset by them! In fact, we are so upset we need their sympathy and understanding. And we need a change *right now!*

Is this too heavy for you to handle right now? I hope not, for if you hear this — really hear it — you will be ready to enter a walk with Him that will bring marvelous new benefits to you . . . direct from His heart.

The witnesses who watch us have many different attitudes about us. Some hope we will lose and some earnestly hope we will win. But they are all watching. We may wish they weren't, but they are.

We *are* surrounded.

If we want to be called a child of God, we will be watched. God will be judged by what people see in us. We probably wish this weren't true, but it is. Knowing that God wants us to be an example before all these spectators may be a heavy thing, but it isn't something we can escape.

When we get into a tight spot and it seems the world is caving in on us, we may let our barriers down. Satan knows this and that is precisely why he probes for weak spots to use to his advantage.

Often we don't have as much trouble with the witnesses who are "out there". It's easy to put our best foot forward for the public. But what about when we close the doors of our homes?

I most often let down all the barriers when I was at home. It was "tea and sympathy time" as I would talk about the terribly rough trip I had just been on. I had to share how I had spoken several times a day, been kept up until midnight, been too exhausted to sleep, and been talked at until my ears ached. I felt I needed to tell my family all about this, so they would know how rough poor ol' dad had it when he was out serving the Lord. Their reaction?

"Why does God treat dad so unfairly?"

You see, their reaction was against God. But what if I were a Christian ditchdigger? The principle is the same. If

117

I'm a ditchdigger and I belong to God, then He is responsible for whatever job I have. He could help me get a better job. He could make me the boss, or even the supervisor of a dozen bosses. But if He doesn't, then my job is the one He has provided for me.

So, if I continue to complain, I'm really telling my family, "God isn't really taking very good care of Dad. He has left him here to do all the dirty work. He has surrounded him with people who don't appreciate him, don't give him the right breaks, don't pay him enough, don't give him enough time off. He promised to supply us with everything we need, but He isn't doing a very good job of it for Dad."

God promises to be always with us, and always to give us what we need at the exact time we need it. The witnesses are watching us to see what kind of God we have.

These witnesses are in our homes. They are the children who often turn their backs on God because they see Him "mistreating" their parents. Perhaps their Christian mother expresses her great burdens a hundred times a day. She doesn't blame God, of course. She blames her husband, her neighbors, her husband's boss, her pastor or the children themselves. She is seen as unhappy. If she were a page from a coloring book, it would say, "Color me blue." God hasn't done anything great for her, so why should the people who watch her be drawn to her God?

Parents, stop a minute and take a look at Jesus. He despised the shame and endured the cross, because He only looked at the finish-line. The cloud of witnesses could only see Him as victorious. Even when He was on the cross, they looked up and said, "Surely this was the Son of God."

God has not placed you on a cross, but He may have a cross for you to bear. He has placed you in the situation He wants you to be in. He has a plan for your life, just as carefully thought out as the plan for His own Son.

True, you have made some decisions that brought you to your present position in life, but your Father could have stopped you.

He could rearrange everything in your life right now if He wanted to. He could elevate every member of your family or reduce them to nothing.

Since you are His child, nothing would be too much bother for Him. But He will do only what He knows is good for the spirit He has placed in you. That spirit is being prepared for eternity.

Have you any idea how long eternity will be? Can you see why it is important that God use everything in your brief life on earth to prepare you to fit into His perfect plan?

God has worked many wonderful healings in my body. The healings helped me to learn things I needed to know about spiritual healing. But at other times, God has done nothing to improve my physical condition, even when I prayed exactly as I had done before. My first reaction was to think, "What am I doing wrong? Why isn't God helping me?"

Discouragement filled my thoughts as the sin which clings so closely tried to pull me down. Undoubtedly this was seen and felt by everyone who knew me. Their faith had to be unfavorably influenced. The Spirit eventually helped me to understand that I would profit by *not* being healed right away.

This didn't mean that God didn't want to heal me. It meant that I had to learn something first. He was preparing me for time and eternity, rather than for the temporary world I'm now living in.

You may never have experienced a supernatural physical healing and are tempted to think all kinds of discouraging thoughts like:

"Maybe I'm not good enough, maybe God doesn't heal people in this life, maybe . . . "

The point is — don't be discouraged, or even think a discouraging thought, when you aren't healed or prayers don't seem to be answered *right now*. Believe that God is using the situation to work something good in you.

Believe that God is using your present situation to bring His best into your life. Don't be upset when people say you are blaming God for your lack of faith. You aren't blaming Him — you are believing God that He is using your problem to work out something good ... in His own perfect time.

Remember, in Hebrews 11, God chose Old Testatment examples of men and women who *did* believe and trust God. How do we believe when the answer doesn't come?

Faith *is our answer*.

God is healing me — even if He does it through death. This is receiving *now* and being honored by God in *eternity*.

As the Spirit helped me to understand this, in my heart, I entered into new peace. The miracle of believing *without seeing* became far more powerful in me than miracles of healing I had experienced. This new peace began to reign in me even when some of the witnesses surrounding me tried to steal my peace.

I keep learning that, no matter what other humans do, I can believe God is working in their actions (or lack of actions) to bless me. And I keep on learning and learning. Maybe His plan is for us to keep learning in eternity!

As I have held back my tongue from complaining to others about my problems, I have become more aware of His Presence. I have sensed His Spirit imparting new strength within, my testimony has grown stronger. He is answering my prayers more. And my prayers are less and less for me and more for those He wants to help through me.

I've become less eager to want to tell others about my great burdens. I consider them more and more as God's will for me, to help me learn something I need to know.

I still occasionally catch myself telling someone about "my problem", hoping for a little sympathy. But then I remember who I am and what my Father has promised to do for me. My spirit within is strengthened and I want to manifest His Spirit by what I feel inwardly, and what I say outwardly. My spirit wants to be like Him. My spirit wants to show the world that Jesus is victorious in me.

His Spirit *really* is my Comforter. He bears all my griefs and carries all my sorrows, just as He said He would. He wants to be a light in me that shines for all the world to see.

I'm glad I am not required to be the strong one. I'm only to believe that His strength is enough for me, simply because I can take Him at His Word — "My grace is sufficient for thee."

Jesus knew this and rested His case with the Father. No higher nor more merciful court of appeal exists. The Father responded with His perfect care, even though those observing through human eyes tended to question it. But that was because they could not see how He would bring good out of what looked bad. You and I see as though we were looking "through a glass darkly", but our Heavenly Father sees the end from the beginning. He knows what He is doing. The wisest thing you or I can do it to trust Him, and even more so when things look darkest.

Some of the most effective Christians I have ever known have been people who were in great pain or were dying. Instead of looking for sympathy, they were looking for opportunities to tell others (the cloud of witnesses) how good their Father was to them.

This kind of Christian reached me in a way nothing else could. I couldn't resist their devotion to God. I was able to see what God was doing in them. Instead of being afraid of death, they were excited about what lay ahead. They could hardly wait to be in His Presence.

I wanted such a relationship with Him. I needed it. Everything in me wanted something that would give me this kind of strength when my turn came to die.

And then I remembered that these same people had faced daily problems when they were not seriously ill, with exactly the same kind of victory! They were dying as they had lived. I wanted to live as they were dying.

I recently received a letter from a prisoner whose life was changed by such a testimony. It didn't happen overnight, but in God's perfect timing a dramatic change occurred in his life.

He writes, "I am in jail for bank robbery. I'm probably looking at a long time in the pen. Since I've been in here, my girl friend has found out that she is pregnant. I want desperately to marry her ... "

He continues, "I used to curse God, but now I realize how wrong I was. Your book, *Prison to Praise* showed me a lot of things and I have accepted Christ as my Savior. I realize now how wrong I was, being bitter and resentful over what happened to my brother. He had muscular dystrophy all of his life, but he served God with all of his strength. He was taken (died) by this disease, and other complications, during an operation for an ulcer, along with pneumonia.

"He made a lot of people very happy and his *last words* were, 'I love you, Jesus.' He never doubted God for a minute. I truly want the peace that he had even to the last. At the time I blamed God. Now I see that He has used everything to get through to me."

The widow who gave her mite did not expect to be held up as an example of giving. In her wildest dreams, she would never have thought that her example would be broadcast around the world. Her gift seemed insignificant in her own eyes, but God honored her gift. He saw the intent of her heart.

Jesus responded differently to the man who took his one talent and hid it! Jesus said if he had used that one talent to the best of his ability, God would have enlarged and multiplied it.

I have seen this happen in my own life over and over. The little natural ability I have could accomplish very little. But as I have given Him what little I have, without complaining over the things I didn't have, He blessed and multiplied that which I gave to Him.

If we hold on to what we have, because we see our needs are so great and our resources are so small, all the while listening to the voice of fear say, "It isn't enough," we lose our reward.

When the young boy offered his few fishes and loaves in the face of overwhelming need, the disciples said, "but what are they among so many?"

Aren't we sometimes like this?

Jesus wants to change this type of thinking in us. He wants us to think in terms of abundance. The young boy is to be our example. He had more faith than all the disciples put together! He didn't worry about what he didn't have. He willingly offered what he did have. And Jesus created an abundance out of his offering.

Offer up what you have and He will multiply it!

If you have even the slightest bit of ability to praise Him, do it. It will be your step of faith.

Don't let *anyone* catch you grumbling or complaining. Everyone around you is complaining! Little do people realize they are doing it for Satan. And that is just what Satan wants.

But God wants some praisers! Praise Him, believing your life is being used for His glory. And it will be ... far beyond what you could ever imagine.

Your life will honor Him ... because it is filled with praise, your joy will draw others to Him. He will heal their diseases, forgive their sins and give them eternal life.

Wouldn't their blessings be worth your giving up the right to complain?

I see the Holy Spirit convincing you that God wants you never again to be unhappy about anything. He releases you from the misguided idea that you must be burdened over your mistakes and those of others.

Instead, you are *now free* to be what He created you for — *to be filled with trust in Him* that nothing and no one could destroy His purpose for your life.

Now, begin expecting the spirit of praise to grow and grow, until it fills your life!

He wants to use you to bless others!

This is real power!

XV

WHY WAS I BORN?

How often have you heard people say, "It's a small world"? The expression generally comes up in the sort of situation when we meet someone for the first time who turns out to be a close acquaintance of a cousin with whom we played during summer vacations in childhood. And it expresses our love of the familiar. We welcome friends and shun strangers.

Most of us try to arrange our lives along these lines. We want to protect ourselves from an alien and awesome world in which we too often feel utterly alone and isolated. The fact is, it's an enormous and frightening world inhabited today by about 4 billion human beings. And modern communications tend in many ways to reinforce this impression. Thanks to the miracle of television even the Tibetans and Afghans are no further away than our living rooms, but that doesn't make them seem much less foreign to us. More than ever, then, we easily begin to feel lost in the shuffle ... little more than a social security number lost in a morass of bureaucratic red tape. It's a world increasingly characterized by a telephone answering machine asking us to "leave your message at the tone".

When faced with fears and difficulties, doubts often come knocking at our door. But we don't have to invite them in and entertain them. Instead we can reflect on some important facts.

1. The Jews fled from Egypt.
   — the Egyptians perished.
2. David fled from Saul.
   — Saul perished.
3. Elijah fled from Jezebel.
   — Jezebel (you guessed it) perished.
   — and Elijah was rewarded with a chariot ride to Heaven!

The Scriptures abound with stories of people who faced overwhelming odds but who found that their greatest fears held no more substance than a vaporous mist momentarily shutting out the sunlight.

God will allow us to experience conflict. For it is only in conflict that He can prove that He meant what He said, "I will never, no never, under any circumstances, ever leave or forsake you."

A remarkable psalm shows how important it is for us to go through difficult experiences while we are in this life. It speaks among other things of those who "go down to the sea in ships". Few things are more awesome or terrifying than the power of any angry sea. People who must endure it aboard ship readily recognize their need for God's help.

"Then they cry unto the Lord in their trouble, and he bringeth them out of their distress." (Ps. 107:27)

If we were always in calm and shallow waters, we would never discover the joy of being delivered from the deep waters. Besides, no merchantman ever turned a profit by staying in the safety of a harbor. The reward is reserved for the sailor who will launch out into the deep and leave the safety of the harbor behind.

Besides, there's little use in trying to hang around in a safe place. God inevitably has ways of either prodding or luring us out into the deep waters where the stakes are high and the rewards are greatest. And He will make sure we stay there — in peril — until we have learned to praise Him!

Verse twenty-two of Psalm 107 declares, "Let them sacrifice the sacrifices of thanksgiving." But that doesn't make sense to us. We want to see God deliver us from each problem *before* we give Him our thanks.

Jesus was out at sea in deep waters, in the midst of a raging storm that frightened even experienced fishermen. But Jesus rested peacefully in His Father's care, because He lived by the word of God, which includes the 107th Psalm.

If you haven't understood, read verse 27, "they reel to and fro and stagger like a drunken man and are at their wit's end." Does that describe how you feel sometimes? It need not, because His calm is available to those who will praise Him *now, in the midst* of the storm.

In the face of life's storms, many people plead and beg for God to intervene. Still the storm continues to rage all around them. Frantic cries for help are not the answer to the problem. Answers lie in what Jesus showed us.

He was calm before the wind and the waves — right in the middle of the problem. The disciples were perturbed. They said, "Don't you even care that we are all about to perish?"

Our problem may seem to be more than we can bear, but it isn't. It is exactly what we need at this time.

Please believe this for your own sake. God will respond to our prayers as we respond to His Son, who said, "Let not your heart be troubled."

I received a beautiful letter from a nurse. What she told me illustrates the beauty that often develops in a life of one who goes through unusual trouble.

Your first book was sent to me November 19, 1971. I remember the date simply because I had been admitted to the hospital for a spinal injury that was pronounced medically hopeless.

I was working for the State Hospital as a student nurse when I did I serious damage to my spine. I spent five weeks in traction — I could not walk.

I was alone and did not even know where my mother and father were. But, because of your praise book, I had beautiful fellowship with the Lord those five weeks.

I was discharged in a wheel chair, but had to return to the hospital in a short time. I was scheduled for very delicate surgery and was told I would never walk again ... a dismal prospect for a nineteen-year-old girl, with dreams and hopes that now seemed to hang by a precarious thread.

As I read your book, I began to *praise God in earnest* for everything, believing, "all things work together for good to them who love the Lord ... " (Rom. 8:28)

When the surgeon requested my surgical consent, I told him I needed forty eight hours to pray. He looked at me with a rather funny expression on his face, but agreed to the time.

When he came back, I told him to do what he felt necessary, but that I *would* walk again.

He asked me how I knew this and I said, "My Heavenly Father told me."

The surgeon actually called in a psychiatrist because he felt that I was not 'being realistic'. I talked to the psychiatrist for two-and-a-half hours. He told the surgeon, "She's quite realistic — you should talk to her more often."

I was out of bed thirteen hours after surgery and with the Lord's strength I have been walking ever since! At first not without a great deal of pain, but as I earnestly praised God for the pain and for the fact that I couldn't walk well (and sometimes not at all), I began to see God's power manifest itself in my life. I was out of the hospital in three weeks and soon resumed my nursing classes.

If I had not learned to praise the Lord, I could very well have been a helpless cripple the rest of my life.

***

I received another letter, regarding a completely different kind of problem. It was filled with defeat instead of praise.

I badly need help or advice. I am guilty of the sin of gluttony.

This thing preys on my mind constantly and I hate myself for it. I also hate the many overweight pounds! I hate the fact that it is sin and that I am grieving the Holy Spirit by it.

Look, I just can't say no to food. The creamier the cakes, the better I like them. Sometimes I eat all day. I am uncomfortable most of the time with that awful stuffed feeling one gets from overeating. The Bible says a gluttonous man won't enter Heaven and brother, I know the Scripture on this subject!

I also know the Scripture says I am not in bondage to anything, but this doesn't apply to me. Because I am in bondage to food! And how!

I have been prayed for time and time again! I have tried fasting. (What a battle this is, with no lasting results.) This seems to be creating a real barrier between God and me.

I am increasingly lazy as a result of being overweight. I am irritable ninety percent of the time and I am tired all of the time! The Scriptures say, "To Him that overcometh, I will give a crown of life," so perhaps I won't even make Heaven. But I do love the Lord and want to please Him. Please, Mr. Carothers, can you help me?

This girl's gluttony was thriving on self-pity. But, more

tragically, she mistakenly thought eternal life depended on something she had to do. The more unhappy she became, the more weight she gained. And the more weight she gained, the more unhappy she became! Her sense of condemnation grew as the pounds mounted.

Problems will never back off because we are unhappy. They thrive on unhappiness! The most powerful enemy of our problems is praise.

Praise puts strength back into diseased bones, jangled nerves and weakened flesh. When we are offering praise, we can actually feel a little spark of hope leap up within, like a surge of power. It is in fact a surge of the greatest power known to man — faith.

A remarkable letter came to me from a woman in prison who was charged with murder. She had received Christ as Savior since coming to the penitentiary. She wrote:

> I am so thankful that in spite of all that has happened in my life, God let me know that He loves me and now my faith and trust in Him are just that much stronger. Even here so many of our prayers have been answered, it's almost too wonderful to be true.
>
> My lawyer came and told me the other day I didn't have a chance. Both my husband and I have been indicted for murder. We are still thankful for so many things and praising Him more every day. The Lord has a plan for us, we know. Now we can tell others what we went through to find Christ as our Savior, and our story will help lead others to Him. The happiness and flow of living water within is just a wonderful, joyous feeling!

In prison, charged with murder, and able to trust and praise God for using this to bring them to Christ! What a testimony! Many people in prison give in to despair because of physical problems and limitations. Others commit suicide.

***

Another illustration is Debbie. She was arrested in June of 1976 and charged with murder. Her family was unable to raise bail so Debbie had to stay in prison until her trial.

While in jail awaiting trial, her mother saw remarkable changes in her. Although she had been raised in a church-going family, faith had not been a very important part of Debbie's life. But now her letters to her mother were full of hope and confidence that she would be exonerated and released from prison as soon as her trial was finished.

Her mother wrote to me saying, "It was almost as though she were a different person. She looked different. She acted different. She was all aglow. She was radiant! She never complained. Truly, there was a change in my daughter — a beautiful, real change."

During the six months waiting for her trial, Debbie became more and more dedicated to serving God regardless of the outcome of her trial.

While awaiting trial, she gave birth to a baby girl. She was offered a twenty year sentence for a lesser offense if she would plead guilty. She refused "the deal" and chose a jury trial instead.

The family's prayers went unanswered and Debbie was found guilty and sentenced to fifty years in prison. Her mother's reaction was, "God, how could *You* let me down? Let Debbie down?"

Debbie wrote to her mother, "Mom, praise God for all things, even that I am going to prison." Her concern was only for her mother and sisters. Her mother wrote, "I was numb and I couldn't hear her." But Debbie continued writing, "Praise God, Mom. Please praise God."

But her mother said, "My daughter was sent to prison for fifty years. How could I praise God for that?" The mother's anguish increased until it was becoming more than she could bear. Instead of being able to comfort her daughter, she says, "I continued to wallow in my nightmare."

Then came Debbie's letter.

"Mom, you aren't the one going to prison. You aren't the one who loved a man who did you wrong. You aren't the one who had to give up your baby for adoption. You aren't the one who'll be confined for the most important years of your life. If this is happening to me and I can still praise the Lord, Mom, what's wrong with you? Please read Merlin Carothers' book, *Prison to Praise*."

Although other friends had recommended that she read *Prison to Praise*, Debbie's mother had never done so. Now she realized Debbie had something she needed. She wrote to me, "When I completed your book, I cried for a long time and then got on my knees and gritted my teeth and said, "God, thank you for my daughter, Debbie. Praise You that Debbie is going to prison. Thank you God for letting my daughter go to prison."

"I could never explain what went on inside my heart," she continued.

"I thought before I got up from the side of my bed that my heart was going to explode. Then an overwhelming peace came. Debbie's testimony has given a 'stale Christian' new hope and a renewed love and zest for our Lord. I never knew this kind of joy could be mine. It's marvelous. He has lifted that heavy burden (Debbie's imprisonment) from my heart and has breathed His Spirit into my life. I shall praise His name forever!"

***

A fifty-five-year-old man wrote to me:

Having been orphaned and passed around a great deal of my childhood, which I took as a round of rejections, I have never been able to believe anyone loved me. Several people tried awfully hard, but deep down I just felt that I wasn't loveable. I also believed for years, intellectually, that God loved me, but it was never *real* to me at all. God has been dealing with me about my past experiences and some other things during the past six weeks or so, but the matter of loving me never came up.

Then one day last week, after reading your book,

Bringing Heaven Into Hell, I was sitting in a restaurant having a cup of coffee and reading the New Testament. All of a sudden, it hit me like a Mack truck! — God loves *me!*

I can't tell you how that hit me! I wanted to run down the street yelling at the top of my lungs, 'HEY, EVERYBODY. GOD LOVES ME!! HE REALLY DOES!'

I know this may sound frightfully silly coming from a fifty-five-year-old man, but I had to restrain myself from doing just that. And I have been bubbling inside ever since. I have never felt so good about anything in my life, and nothing that happens seems to be able to destroy that feeling.

The other day I fell off a ladder onto a cement driveway, and I just laughed and said, "Well, praise the Lord!'

I have never felt so good about the future. I know it is going to be out of sight and the present is beyond anything I've ever experienced in peace and contentment."

When anyone realizes God's love in a very personal way, he has the beginning of a new feeling deep inside that wants to shout, "God, I'm glad I was born!"

Why were we born?

I can tell you.

To acknowledge, receive, and experience the love of God.

XVI

IN ALL THINGS

Praise is a wonderful channel God has provided. Through it He can effectively pour the Presence of His love back into our lives — in order that we might "know that we know, that we know" that He loves us! And, because this is so, we can let Him be in control.

God is ever faithful to provide us with opportunities to grow in faith — to exercise and release our faith through praise. He provided me with just such an opportunity in a real life adventure I shall not soon forget — and which I would not have missed for anything!

***

Mary and I had scheduled a trip to Baja California,

Mexico, with friends in their motor home. We had never driven farther than a few miles across the Mexican border, and, so, the trip promised to be interesting.

I had been sending copies of the Spanish edition of *Prison to Praise* to prisoners all over Mexico, and I felt I needed a better "feel" for the people of Mexico. This trip would provide an excellent opportunity to fulfill that need.

However, as the date for our departure neared, we began to hear some disconcerting things about our friend who would be driving his large motor home for this excursion. I knew he had a vision problem because of a previous eye injury, but I had no idea how serious it was. But, when we learned that several members of his family would never even ride in *any* vehicle he was driving . . . well, we began to get the picture.

And we were now scheduled to take a 1,500 mile trip with him, driving over notoriously dangerous roads. It wasn't until later that we learned how *really* dangerous!

We were caught in a dilemma.

We had promised to make the trip with our friends and I don't break promises. But was this the kind of promise I should keep, when I was responsible to God to take care of my own family?

On the other hand, I knew that, as a child of the King, I should learn to trust Him. He knew the condition of my friend's eyes *long before* I ever made the promise.

Should I trust in God's perfect care or should I listen to the voice of "common sense" and stay home?

I decided to find out exactly what my friend's eyes were like. What a revelation! He was totally blind in one eye and had only 50 percent vision in the other. This meant he had only one-fourth normal vision!

"Lord, now I know for *sure* You wouldn't want me to take my family on a trip like that!"

All I got back from the Lord was, "Trust Me."

"Wouldn't that be like jumping off the top of a building and trusting You to save me?"

"No, it wouldn't," was the only reply.

I realized my friend was driving his motor home everywhere. " . . . must have a legion of angels protecting him," I thought to myself.

"Okay, Lord. We'll go, but it's all in Your hands now."

***

The roads in the northern part of Baja California are excellent. We headed south from San Diego, crossed the border at San Ysidro, and entered Tijuana. It was smooth sailing down the coast and through Ensenada, as my friend breezed along with apparently no problems. It began to look as if our fears had been groundless.

Then the roads began to narrow.

The level plains gradually turned into mountains! The roads were just wide enough for two cars to pass . . . if neither car had an extra coat of paint!

Just off the edge of the paved road there was often a twelve inch drop-off and then about twelve inches of soil. Beyond this point, it was over the edge and straight down! A sheer drop into space — without benefit of guardrail! Absolutely nothing to keep you from sailing over the edge if you should happen to miss the next sharp curve! To our dismay, my friend sang and drove as if he were on a six-lane highway.

He surely seemed to be enjoying the ride. I had to agree it was getting exciting, but I couldn't say I was enjoying it!

At times, I sat in the front and watched and prayed — mostly prayed. When watching became too nerve-racking, I would get into the back of the motor home, lie down and pray. "Pray without ceasing" took on new meaning. My faith seemed so very, very weak. At times I felt we surely must have left the road and were sailing over the edge of the mountain!

Did I hear a small, still voice say, "Oh thou of little faith? . . . "

"Lord, don't let me doubt You now. We belong to You. Nothing could happen to us unless You permitted it. Forgive my fear."

For a time I would be cheered up and even start singing.

But then we would veer around a sharp bend and the song I sang to keep my spirits up, would get stuck in my throat as I held my breath and took a tighter grip on my vascillating faith! One look at Mary told me that she too was learning to "pray without ceasing" in a new and personal way!

One evening we were deep into a mountainous area when we were caught in a real downpour. I urged my friend to stop and park, on the very edge of the mountain, if need be. But he just kept going. It became pitch black outside and the windshield wipers began to work rather erratically. With 20-20 vision in both eyes I could hardly see anything. How could he even see to keep us on the road?

Then he gave me a portable light that operated off the cigarette lighter and asked me to roll down the window on my side and shine the light on the road ahead. This definitely improved the field of vision, but imagine the plight we were in. Going down a narrow mountain road with no guardrail, windshield wipers that barely worked and a driver with only a fourth of his vision!

At one point our friend found a place about seven feet wide and pulled the motor home over to the side of the road, but it was dangerously near the sheer drop-off.

It had continued to pour the rain for some time and we hadn't seen another car for miles. There was nothing left in sight, but mountains straight up on one side of us, and a drop off on the other side ... straight down!

Mary climbed out of the motor home, sat down on the edge of the road and said, "I'm not getting back in! I'm sitting right here until it gets light and this rain stops!"

I was certainly inclined to agree with her, but I had visions of the vehicle sliding off the edge of the mountain during the night!

"Lord, what now?"

All I could hear from Him was, "Trust Me."

And so in my best "head-of-the-home" voice of authority, I told Mary we had to get back in and "keep going until we can get to a safer place."

Down the dark and winding mountain road we continued. After about forty-five minutes, that seemed more like forty-five hours, we reached the bottom.

I still believe God must have had 10,000 angels all around that motor home to keep it from becoming airborne off the edge of one of those perilous mountain roads!

As we continued our journey our friend kept revealing how little he really could see. At times, he would say, "Hey Merlin, look ahead for me and see if I can pass that truck up ahead."

My first reaction was, "Look ahead! What do you mean? You're driving!"

But then I came to realize that he couldn't see far enough ahead to tell if anyone was coming in the opposite direction!

How God stretched and stretched our faith.

"Trust Me," had been His continual assurance.

"Yes, Lord. But am I trusting You or just being plain stupid?" had crossed my mind more than once.

Such questions often aren't easy to answer. I'm definitely not recommending that you ride in vehicles with drivers who can barely see the road ahead. This was an exceptional experience and God purposed to use it to teach me to trust Him.

I'm not eager to go through the same experience again, but I learned many, many things on that trip that I wouldn't trade for a month of Sundays lounging in my easy chair! And we did thoroughly enjoy the fellowship with our friends.

This point is this. When situations are such that our faith is on the line and we must trust Him, He won't fail us.

"None who have faith in God will ever be disgraced for trusting in Him. " (Ps.25:3, TLB)

Sometimes He has to allow us to get into a situation where we can't see our way clearly. And sure disaster seems to loom just ahead. Having tried everything else to no avail, we surrender ourselves to Him by an act of our will — and start praising Him for everything, just as it is. Somewhat like the person who tries every way he can to solve a problem without success and then says to himself, "Maybe I'd better try what I've been hearing about this praise business . . . ."

You might jokingly say, "Oh, it's come to that, has it?" The truth is, it must come to that — and the sooner the better.

We may not always understand fully how it works, any more than how light floods the room when the switch is flipped. The important thing is — it works. The power is there, waiting to be turned on.

Think of praise as a force more powerful than gravity. I don't really understand completely how gravity works, but I know it does. And although I don't completely understand how the power of praise works, I know it does.

When Jesus walked on the water, He withstood the gravity force of a planet 25,000 miles in circumference and weighing thousands of billions of tons. He did this by His trust in God.

Since praise is faith in action, praise is trust that God can use even gravity for our good, if necessary. Praise that works believes that God will use all the force of the universe to make everything work for our good if we believe Him.

God used a dream to dramatically illustrate this to a woman who had read all of my books. She wrote to me:

"Have you ever visualized 'the car of your dreams?' The Lord showed me 'the car of my dreams' in a dream. It was a very special car — special because the Lord used it to convey a vivid picture of His provision to meet my personal needs in an uncertain future.

"In my dream, my children and I were in this beautiful car — it looked so perfect. We had 'arrived' to be riding through life in such luxury. Somehow I knew that we were at the very mountaintop of success, and this luxurious car symbolized it all. In fact, we were on a vacation, traveling through some beautiful mountainous terrain. The view was breath-taking.

"Suddenly, the car began to roll backwards. Then I discovered the fatal flaw in my 'dream car'. It had no brakes! Directly behind us lay treacherous curves, a car out of control and no brakes!

"But a strange thing happened. Instead of panicking, I began to praise the Lord. And I found that as I continued to increase my praise to Him, the car began to slow down. The car eventually reached the bottom of this dangerous, winding road ... and gently rolled to a full stop!

"I awoke with a sigh of relief. It had only been a dream! But even as I realized this, I *also* realized the Lord was reaffirming the importance of praise in my life.

"If I kept praising Him, when things looked the very worst, He would take over and everything would be okay.

"Facing a marriage that was falling apart and fearful of the future for myself and my children, the Lord showed me He would be our security as long as I kept praising Him ... for we were all in the same boat ... or 'car', I guess I should say.

"He reminded me of the 91st Psalm ... 'because I have made the Lord, which is my refuge, even the most High, my habitation ...' He promised me His constant care — even as a mother hen gathers her little ones under her wing of protection — and somehow praise is the energizing, activating power which makes this a daily, living reality — even moment by moment."

***

The car in the dream is a lot like life. Everything looks perfect. Many of life's dreams and aspirations seem to have been realized. We have arrived at the mountaintop of success. Then the bottom drops out.

What do we do when everything is suddenly out of our control, like a car without brakes careening towards certain disaster? How are we going to put the brakes on our problems when our own resources are suddenly bankrupt!?

If your life seems to be getting out of control, like a runaway car without any brakes, you need some "praise brakes". In fact, the Lord may have allowed you to be just where you are so that you would *have* to trust Him.

You may not like the "car" (situation) in which you are

riding, but it has been custom-made for His purposes in your life. In it you can ride with the security that you will safely arrive at the destination He has for you — His perfect will — when you are willing to trust Him enough to use those "praise brakes" — to keep praising Him in ALL things.

God's requirements are not difficult. One of His requirements is that we would rejoice in Him *continually*. Continually means just that — continually.

We have become geared to question everything we read, hear or even see. We have been told one car, soap or toothpaste is better than any other, only to be confronted by a different advertisement asserting even more strenuously that another product is absolutely the best!

Politicians make conflicting statements and, in our confusion, we are unable to decide what is really true, consequently, we adopt an attitude of "who knows what's right about anything?" Or, as Pontius Pilate asked Jesus, "What is truth?"

Isn't that the spirit that infects the times we live in?

We distrust our government, the values that have kept our society stable, and even the quality of merchandise our dwindling dollar can purchase. The integrity that stands behind it all seems increasingly questionable.

Unfortunately this attitude can influence our attitude towards God ... towards His Word.

We hear what Scripture says, but seem to let it pass in one ear and out the other without permitting it to speak to us and to change our way of living. And Satan is right there, slyly whispering, "who knows what God really thinks about anything? Did God really say? ... "

Then, when we read that we are to give thanks in all things, we can't decide if He *really* means all things.

Children are notorious for always being unsure what their mom or dad has told them to do. A child can easily disobey a parent and then rationalize the disobedience by thinking, "I'm not really sure what dad said."

They aren't sure because they don't want to be.

The desire to do what the child wants to do becomes

stronger than his desire to obey.

But we are told that we must put away "childish ways," if we are to be spiritually mature. We *can* decide exactly what God said and meant and intended. Then we can set our will to obey Him.

We can praise Him for *all* things — simply because He said to. This can be the beginning of order in the midst of the confusion that is all around us.

As Christians we have a glorious opportunity to show our love for God by obeying Him. So we don't have to try to decide what He meant when He told us to praise Him for all things — continually. Just decide what "continually" means.

Don't evade the word. Don't claim not to know what He means. Look it up in Webster's dictionary if you must — it's very clear. It means always, at all times — and as God's Word points out, even "sacrificially", if need be. (Heb.13:15)

It may seem easier to be sad, worried, angry, lonely or fearful, but God has told His children to rejoice *in Him* always.

"In *all things* give thanks, for *this is the will of God for you* in Christ Jesus." (IThess. 5:18)

We cannot escape His will.

We may disobey, but that won't change His will!

A woman became so depressed that she decided the demands of family responsibilities were too great for her. In confusion of mind and with a spirit submerged in deep depression, she lost control. In a moment of insanity she shot and killed her husband and two children.

A fellow pastor and I visited her in prison. We told her that, in spite of all that had happened, God wanted her to rejoice . . . to offer the sacrifice of praise. And in this case it had to be a sacrifice, for it was beyond her understanding to see how she should praise the Lord for the grotesque consequences of her wicked act.

And there in that miserable section of prison, reserved for the criminally insane, I could hardly bring myself to believe this woman should rejoice. But God's laws do not bend to fit our circumstances ... or our misgivings.

My fellow pastor kept going to visit this woman and kept encouraging her to praise God for her past, present and future, and to believe that He could take her terrible act and work something good out of it.

Some Christians I know would be horrified ... "the very idea!"

"How could God do that?"

But God did.

As this woman praised God, her own life began to change. A new-found peace replaced her total despair.

Oh, yes, she despaired over the unalterable act she had committed. Her family was gone. She had repeatedly attempted to take her own life, as the reality and finality of the past had progressively sunk in.

But now, God somehow clothed the stark reality of her life in His love, compassion and forgiveness, and miraculously she became able to smile ... cautiously at first. Finally, she was able to rejoice in the wonder of God's forgiveness.

Miracle after miracle began to happen.

The prison psychiatrist told us this woman has brought life back into people whom he had thought to be emotionally and spiritually beyond hope. Many have come to a positive, clear knowledge of salvation through faith in Christ. And members of her own family have also come to know Christ.

The list could go on and on.

I know that God's law is firm. Whatever our past was, our present is, or our future threatens to be, He wants us to rejoice and trust Him. The choice is either to obey or to disobey.

The decision is up to you and to me.

Think for a moment about the first disciples.

When they were imprisoned, they could easily have centered their attention on their misfortune. Sleeping on damp stone floors and spending countless hours with only cold grey walls and hungry rats as companions would tend to discourage most of us.

These men were continually faced with the prospect of death by fire, crucifixion or lions. In fact, it is believed that every disciple, except John the Younger, was cruelly executed.

But they did not dwell *on* their problems.

They rejoiced and were victorious *over* their problems.

And they kept exhorting those outside of prison to rejoice!

We can follow their example.

God's Word says we must!

Meditate on how the joy of twelve ordinary men has influenced the world for two thousand years!

For more information about Merlin Carothers
and his ministry, write to:

Foundation of Praise
Box 2518
Escondido
California 02025
USA